reunited nation?

reunited nation?

American politics beyond the 2020 election

Michael A. Ashcroft

First published in Great Britain in 2021 by
Biteback Publishing Ltd, London
Copyright © Michael A. Ashcroft 2021

Michael A. Ashcroft has asserted his right under the Copyright, Designs and Patents Act 1988 to be identified as the author of this work.

All rights reserved. No part of this publication may be reproduced, stored in a retrieval system or transmitted, in any form or by any means, without the publisher's prior permission in writing.

This book is sold subject to the condition that it shall not, by way of trade or otherwise, be lent, resold, hired out or otherwise circulated without the publisher's prior consent in any form of binding or cover other than that in which it is published and without a similar condition, including this condition, being imposed on the subsequent purchaser.

Every reasonable effort has been made to trace copyright holders of material reproduced in this book, but if any have been inadvertently overlooked the publisher would be glad to hear from them.

ISBN 978-1-78590-680-0

10 9 8 7 6 5 4 3 2 1

A CIP catalogue record for this book is available from the British Library.

Contents

Introduction — vii

The 2020 election (briefly) explained — 1

The Biden mandate — 11

A reunited nation? — 31

The Trump conundrum — 59

Methodological note — 85

About Lord Ashcroft — 87

Introduction

ON 6 JANUARY 2021, supporters of Donald Trump marched from his "Save America" rally to storm the US Capitol as the two Houses of Congress met to confirm his election defeat. For many, the spectacle was shocking but not all that surprising: the predictable culmination of a terrible presidency that the voters ended after a single term, wishing they had never allowed it to begin.

But the story of the contest between Trump and Joe Biden is more complicated than that, and its repercussions more important. If the 2016 election will stand as one of the defining political events of the century, its successor in 2020 was in many ways at least as remarkable: the supposedly unpopular President winning more votes than any previous Republican nominee, losing only to the candidate with the most votes ever.

Four years ago I published *Hopes and Fears*, my account of the election in which Americans chose Donald Trump with their eyes wide open. Here, drawing on my research throughout the Trump years and during the 2020 campaign, I examine how the voters reacted to his presidency and how they came to replace him. For all the drama that took place between the defeat of one President and the inauguration of the next, this analysis still stands.

Given the "polling miss" of November 2020, readers might be sceptical of any study based on opinion surveys. If so, I don't blame you, but the fact that pre-election polls did not foresee the candidates' relative vote shares, especially in battleground states, does not mean that polling has no value.

One reason the research described in this book is a good basis for analysis is that rather than the usual horse-race question – who are you going to vote for? – we asked people how likely they were to vote for each candidate on a 100-point scale, allowing for more nuance than the traditional question. Combining each voter's answers with their favourability towards their preferred candidate on a separate 100-point scale, we were able to identify groups of Biden and Trump enthusiasts whose balance closely reflected the result of the election. This was based on a sample of more than 20,000 Americans – ten or even twenty times the size of most published polls – which helps with our main aim of comparing in detail the characteristics and priorities of different kinds of voters.

Not only that, the study draws on four years of research conducted as part of my *Ashcroft in America* project. As well as periodic polls with a combined sample well over 100,000, this work has included focus groups in a total of nineteen states with people of all backgrounds and political persuasions. Having crossed the country to listen to the widest and truest range of opinion that we can, I think we can claim to have assembled a robust account of the electorate in the Trump years, the movements that brought about both his election and his defeat, and the implications for the future.

To begin with the winner: what lay behind Joe Biden's record haul of more than 81 million votes, 15 million more than Hillary Clinton, his Democratic predecessor? Even more than usual, this election was not so much a choice between two candidates as it was a referendum on the incumbent. More than nine in ten Trump enthusiasts were voting *for* the sitting President, and more than a quarter of his opponents were voting to get rid of him. This was especially true of previous Trump supporters switching to Biden. In other words, as far as many voters were concerned, Biden had one job – to remove Donald Trump from the White House. In that sense, he will go down in history as the first President to fulfil his mandate on the day of his inauguration.

The problem will come with whatever he decides to do for an encore. As with all successful political movements, Biden's electoral coalition is far from being a monolithic bloc. Its foundation is the Democratic base, many of whose members yearned for a more liberal, progressive direction and found the compromise of nominating an established moderate quite agonising. Many of them hoped that Biden's victory would, in fact, usher in a much more radical Democratic era than might have been suggested by the new President's record in Washington or his reassuringly temperate campaign style. These were joined by a group of new voters, younger and more ethnically diverse, who were opposed to Trump and all his works and were particularly driven to address racial injustice.

Then there is a much more moderate set of voters who wish above all for a calmer, less acrimonious form of politics. Less inclined to dismiss the Trump years out of hand, they were more likely than most to prefer a President who creates a more civil political climate even if they sometimes disagree with him, rather than a President who does the right thing even if it is divisive. If they had doubts about Biden it was over his age and health, and the prospect that Speaker Pelosi would, in the words of one concerned citizen, invoke the Twenty-Fifth Amendment to "remove his ass, and Kamala will be President." What they wanted was not a Green New Deal but a bit of peace and quiet. The potential for conflict and disappointment within the ranks of Biden backers is obvious.

The storming of the Capitol will also prompt some Democrats to think Hillary Clinton had been proved right about her opponents being a "basket of deplorables." It will be easier to delegitimise Trump's voters – however appalled they may have been by the event – than to address the genuine concerns that drove them, sometimes reluctantly, to elect him in the first place.

Though many will have been dismayed at the way it ended, this election was not exactly a repudiation of Donald Trump's presidency. It's a funny sort of repudiation that takes the form of a higher vote share and 11 million more votes. Whatever Trump was offering, there is clearly a huge market for it – something that becomes more important to understand as his reputation implodes. So what were his voters buying?

Looking back at what he did and what his supporters have told us about his appeal over four years of research, I think the list looks something like this (we might call them the Seven Tenets of Trumpism): an enduring belief in American exceptionalism; conviction that constitutional freedoms are important and need defending; a positive view of American life and the opportunities it offers; rejection of political correctness and identity politics; belief in business, low taxes and deregulation; wariness of multilateralism and support for an assertive and independent foreign policy; and – crucially – willingness to tolerate a high degree of friction in politics in the cause of advancing these principles.

This final point leads to a question central to the Republican Party's future: how far can these tenets be disentangled from the 45th President himself? Halfway through his term I asked what would be most remembered about it in twenty years' time; the top answer was "the way Donald Trump has gone about doing the job." Could there be such a thing as Trumpism without Trump?

It has been a recurring theme in our research that many voters drew a distinction between Trump's personality on the one hand and his actions on the other. One in three of our Trump enthusiasts told us they approved of what he had done as President but disapproved of his character and personal conduct. From before he was first elected, people have told us that his antics were a price worth paying for the changes and policies they wanted.

The question of whether he would have won again if he had been less provocative and belligerent is really academic – it amounts to asking if Donald Trump would have done better if he were less like Donald Trump. But an important point that it would be easy to overlook is that two thirds of his supporters said they approved of both his actions *and* the way he conducted himself. That is not to say that most will not have been horrified as events unfolded on 6 January. But for most of his presidency, what others saw as his outrageous behaviour was not just part of the package but part of the appeal – a feature, not a bug. Many of these voters loved having a President who said exactly what he thought and sent Hollywood liberals into a frenzy. They also appreciated having an outsider who set out to drain the Washington swamp, even if he ended up becoming mired in it.

Powerful as it was, this proposition ended up losing. What, then, is the lesson for the Republican Party? For some, the whole Trump era, not just its final few weeks, was an aberration that the GOP should put behind it. But the party cannot simply take its current voting coalition – the biggest it has ever assembled – and trade it in for a different one. Over the past forty years, the Democratic Party's base of support has in economic terms grown steadily more upscale, while the Republicans have become the party of rural and small-town America. The task the Republicans now have is to hold together that base of support, and even expand back into the suburbs and cities themselves.

To say that President Trump's performance since the election has made this task harder would be an understatement of colossal proportions. Those who want it to remain "Donald Trump's Republican Party" (as Don Junior had it at the fateful rally) might try the patience of mainstream Republicans beyond endurance: being uncouth on Twitter is one thing, inciting insurrection is altogether another. But those who want a Trump-free future for the GOP must find a way of distancing themselves from him while holding onto the millions – minus the extremist minority – that he brought into the Republican fold. There is a serious question as to whether the party will continue to exist in its current form.

Yet there is much in the Trump offering that the Republicans can build on. The idea that America is different from other countries and offers unique opportunities and rewards for those prepared to work for them is not only a potent and attractive idea; it can also be a very inclusive one. The problem was that over the last four years, for too many voters, it didn't feel that way. When Donald Trump talked about making America great again, it was often heard as trying to turn back the clock or making America great only for certain kinds of people. Whoever takes the message forward over the next four years, that is what needs to change: call it a strategy of inclusive exceptionalism. At the same time, though friction is inevitable, there needs to be a place in the centre-right coalition for people who value civility and do not want government to feel like a permanent rollercoaster.

It was striking that as Congress resumed its certification of the results after the rude interruption, the energy drained from the objectors, with a number of Senators and Representatives making firmly bipartisan speeches. But for the longer term, hopes of a new age of unity and harmony are surely forlorn. If President Trump did nothing to soothe the country's divisions, nor did he create them. They were there before he descended the Trump Tower escalator to announce his candidacy in 2015, and they will be there long after he has left the scene. As is clear from what follows, Americans disagree over far more than the qualities of one man. But that's what politics is all about.

Michael Ashcroft
January 2021

The 2020 election (briefly) explained

FOR THOSE WHO EXPECTED Joe Biden to win in 2020, the working hypothesis went something like this. Donald Trump's base was famously loyal and had stuck with him throughout the four years of his presidency, but some of his 2016 voters had fallen away, usually because they were disappointed at the way he had conducted himself in office or handled the Covid pandemic. Crucially, these were not being replaced with converts to the Trumpian cause: the President had surely not managed to add to his voting coalition. Meanwhile, unlike in 2016, the Democrats had nominated a candidate whom voters did not find actively off-putting. A combination of higher Democrat turnout, switchers from the Trump camp, and a wave of support from people who had not turned out in 2016 but were appalled at Trump's presidency would see Biden into the White House by a very comfortable margin. In other words, Trump's position was less strong, and the Democrat nominee's less weak, than had been the case four years earlier.

One of these assumptions was wrong – a lesson which has implications for how we understand not just this election but the future of American politics.

To the surprise of many and the dismay of some, Trump did add to his 2016 vote. Not only that, he gained around twice as many voters as he lost. According to my survey of 20,000 voters conducted during October, those who put their chances of voting for Trump higher than for any other candidate having stayed home or voted for Clinton or a third party in 2016 outweighed 2016 Trumpers who now leaned towards Biden or not voting at all by more than two to one.

Nor were these new voters all from the same mould as his 2016 base. As we saw from the exit polls, while Biden won comfortably among women, younger voters, minorities and those with college degrees, when it came to race and gender, he did better than Hillary Clinton only among white men. Trump received the biggest share of non-white voters of any Republican candidate since Richard Nixon in 1960. All told, he received not only some 74 million votes – 11 million more than in 2016 – but a higher share of the vote than four years previously.

The fact that the outcome of the election was ultimately as expected despite Trump's unforeseen surge was simply that Biden did even better, as this graphic illustrates. Trump and Biden 'enthusiasts' are defined here as people who both said they were more likely to vote for that candidate on a 100-point scale than any other candidate, and in a separate question on how positive or negative they felt about each candidate gave their man a score of 75 or above out of 100. This combination has proved a more reliable measure of identifying a candidate's actual voters than a simple voting-intention question.

On this definition, 2016 non-voters who became enthusiasts for Biden or Trump in 2020 went to Biden by around three to two. Those who voted for third-party candidates four years ago but became enthusiasts for one of the main candidates broke for Biden by around two to one. And those switching between the two main parties – even though there were relatively few of these overall – were three times as likely to go from being a Trump voter to a Biden enthusiast as they were to become a Trump enthusiast having voted for Clinton in 2016.

The upshot was that while some 80% of Trump's 2020 enthusiasts had backed him in 2016, only two thirds of Biden enthusiasts had voted for Clinton four years earlier. He won with more than 81 million votes – the highest ever total for a presidential candidate, and over 15 million more than Hillary Clinton in 2016 – and a share of 51%, three points higher than his Democratic predecessor.

High expectations

Both sides went into the election expecting to win. My survey found more than nine out of ten Trump enthusiasts expecting the President to be re-elected, including more than half who thought he would win by a wide margin. Almost as many Biden enthusiasts thought the opposite would happen.

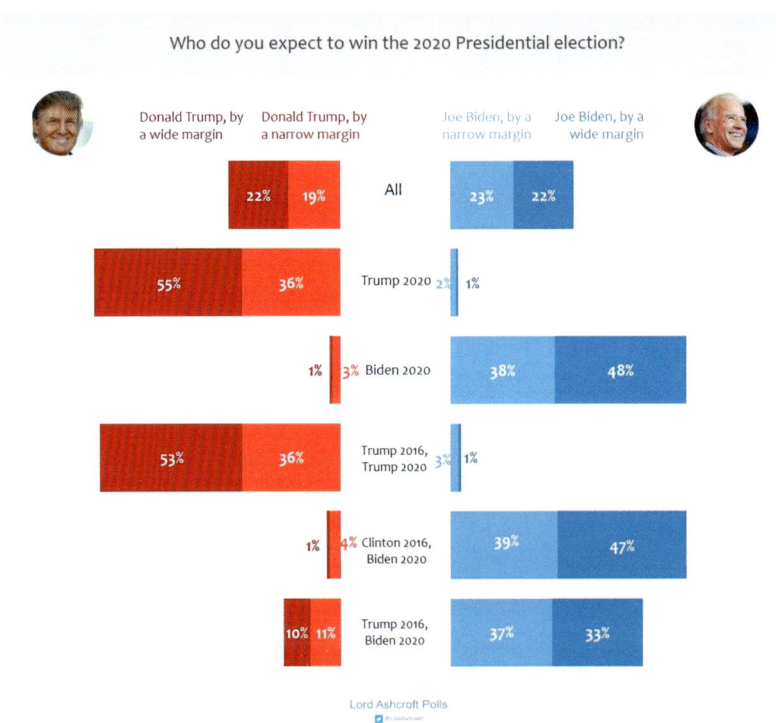

How they voted

As for how they cast their ballots, my survey found just over one third of Biden enthusiasts saying they would vote by mail. This was more than double the proportion of Trump enthusiasts, the great majority of whom were intending to vote in person on the day.

The 2020 election (briefly) explained

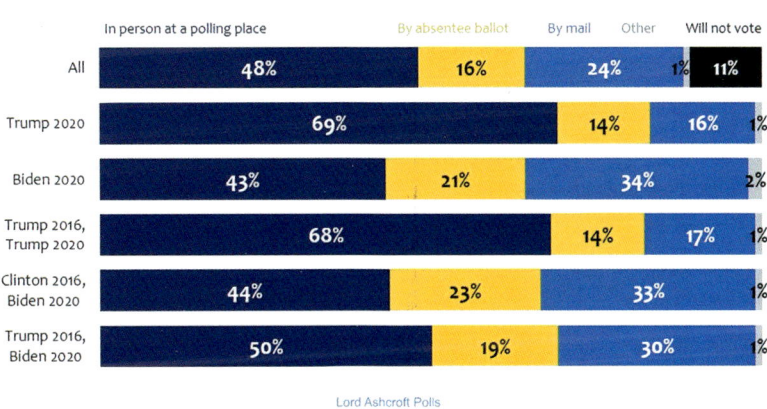

This being the case, it may be that the biggest effect of the Covid pandemic on the presidential election was not the controversy over the administration's handling of the crisis but the explosion of postal voting that it brought about.

Democracy in action?

When it came to the integrity of the election, we found only just over half of voters saying they were confident it would be conducted fairly, and that the person sworn in as President in January would be the rightful winner. Only one in five said they were completely confident that this would be the case. Three in ten said they were not confident at all – a view that was especially prevalent among those describing themselves as socialist (47%), libertarian (45%), and those for whom talk radio was the main source of news (39%).

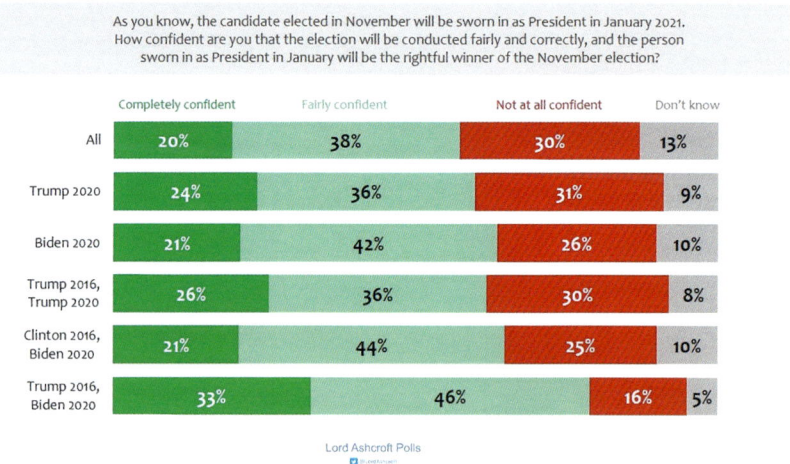

At this stage, there was little to choose between Trump and Biden enthusiasts when it came to confidence in the process. The two groups did differ, however, on what the explanation would be if the result went against them. At the time of our survey in October, it was Biden enthusiasts who were the most likely to say that their defeat would be down to "a systematic effort to rig the outcome of the election."

Trump supporters were more likely to say they would blame media bias in the event of a Biden victory. For them, the campaign had brought a prime example of such bias in the shape of the Hunter Biden email scandal – the claim that messages found on his laptop implicated Joe Biden's son, and potentially the Democratic nominee himself, in corruption involving a Ukrainian energy company. The story was ignored by the main TV news networks and Twitter suspended the account of the *New York Post*, the paper that broke the story. "It's starting to feel like China," complained one Republican-leaning voter. "The more they shut those stories down on social media, the more likely I am to believe that there's truth to it." Others felt the one-sided nature of political coverage was now glaringly obvious: "If Donald Trump can be cross-examined about his taxes, about when he takes his coffee, then Joe Biden can be asked whether or not the family's getting kickbacks from foreign countries." One thing was for sure, they felt: "If this story were about Trump it would be absolutely non-stop. You couldn't get away from it; it would be everywhere." The media was "stirring the pot in one direction only."

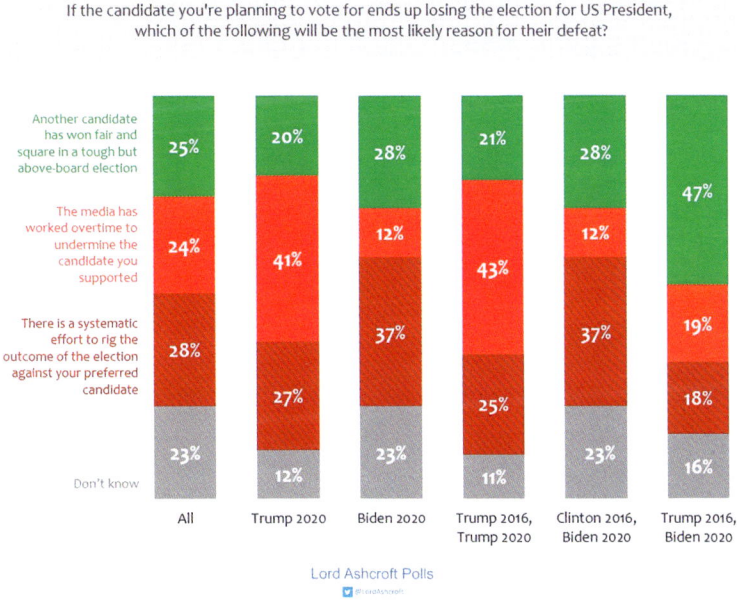

The reaction that Trump supporters said they would have to defeat follows a similar pattern to 2016, but for his opponents it represents a marked shift in opinion. In 2016, nearly half of Democrats said they would accept the result as being above-board even if they lost, compared to 28% now; at the same time, the proportion saying defeat would be down to foul play has doubled.

Only a quarter of voters overall said that if their preferred candidate failed to win, they would have lost fair and square. Notably, 2016 Trump voters now leaning to Biden were among the most confident in the propriety of the outcome, with 47% saying they would accept defeat as the rightful result.

Although many in our pre-election focus groups shared President Trump's professed concerns about the security of mail-in ballots, most of these were worried about straightforward chaos rather than foul play. "If you think about how mail gets lost all the time, votes are going to be showing up in December," said one Florida voter. "Is there going to be a scandal like the hanging chads?" Another in Wisconsin told us, "My father has been dead for ten years, my mother has been dead for five years, and I got applications for their ballots. That's not right. If it's happening to me, it's happening everywhere."

Contest or concede?

We asked those leaning towards Trump and Biden what they would like to see their candidate do – and what they thought they would actually do – in the event that the election result went narrowly against them. Trump enthusiasts were more likely than not to say they would want to see their man contest the result as far as he could in the event of a narrow defeat, with only one in three saying they would prefer him to concede and allow an orderly transition of power.

Notably, however, Biden enthusiasts were even less willing to see their candidate concede than Trump supporters. A clear majority of them said they would want to see the Democrat contest the result if Trump won narrowly, though 2016 Trump voters now leaning towards Biden were more likely than not to say they would prefer to see the Democrat throw in the towel if he lost a close race.

Biden enthusiasts were also more likely to want to see Biden contest a close defeat than to think he would actually do so. The reverse was true for Trump enthusiasts. They were both more ready than Biden supporters to see their candidate concede and more likely to think Trump would contest the result than to say they wanted him to.

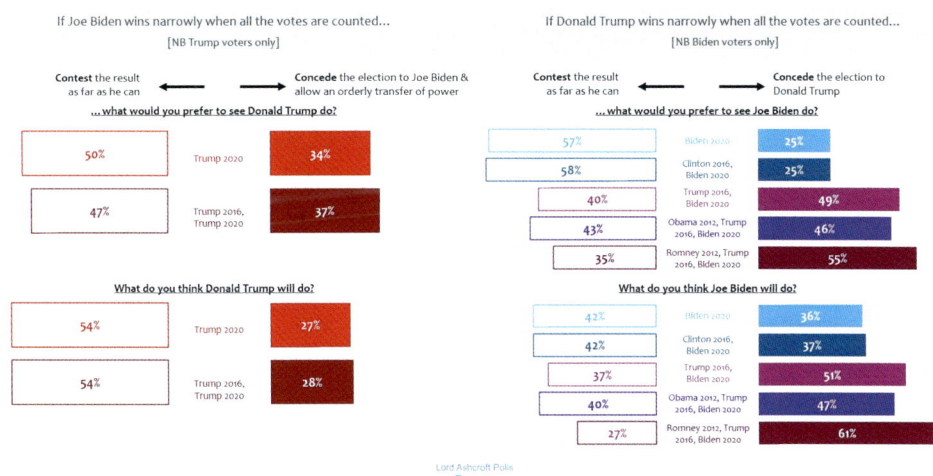

Our focus group participants agreed that Trump was the more likely to challenge a defeat, and some felt this would be the right thing to do in some circumstances. "If it's a blowout, a landslide, then suck it up and take the loss," said one supporter. "But if it's close, why did they give Gore a recount back then and not him?"

Biden was thought more likely to accept defeat, though many thought he would still challenge a Trump victory – although "I don't think Biden would put up the exact same stink as Trump. He would be quieter about it, more respectful. I don't think he would sit there and say 'boo-hoo, poor me' and make the spectacle that Trump is going to make if the roles are reversed."

Many on both sides were worried about the consequences of a long dispute over the results. "In the present situation with all the protests we have, it could easily come to riots," one worried. "I think there might be riots no matter who wins." Even so, each side thought the other was more likely to cause trouble. For those leaning towards Biden, Trump supporters were "more cult-like. Look at QAnon. And there are so many people who believe Trump is their saviour." The arrest of a gang intent on kidnapping the Governor of Michigan was also mentioned in support of this view. But for Republicans, "picketing the streets, protests, I don't see us doing that. They're burning down buildings in Seattle and Portland. I don't remember us rioting in the street when Obama was elected."

Waverers could see fanatics on both sides: "If Trump wins, it will embolden the extremists to go even further to the extreme. And if Biden wins, the pitchforks are going to come out. It's going to be one of the two."

The Biden mandate

WITH MORE THAN 81 million votes, Joe Biden is the most successful presidential candidate in American history. He is only the fifth nominee in the last century to unseat an incumbent President – let alone a President who managed to increase his own vote tally by 11 million. What was this record-breaking electoral coalition voting for?

The Trump referendum

For many voters, including many of his own, the 2020 election was not about Joe Biden at all. Instead, it was a referendum on Donald Trump. In my October survey, 99% of Trump enthusiasts said they approved of the job he had done as President, including 70% who approved strongly. On the other side, 94% of Biden enthusiasts disapproved, 84% doing so strongly.

More than nine out of ten Trump enthusiasts said they would be voting mainly *for* the incumbent President, but the same was not true among his opponents. Although they were more likely to vote for Biden than for any other candidate and gave him a favourability rating of at least 75 out of 100, nearly a quarter of Biden enthusiasts said they would be voting mainly to get rid of Donald Trump. The figure was even higher among those who did not habitually vote for Democrats: only just over half of those leaning to Biden having backed Trump or stayed at home in 2016 said they would be voting positively for the Democrat challenger.

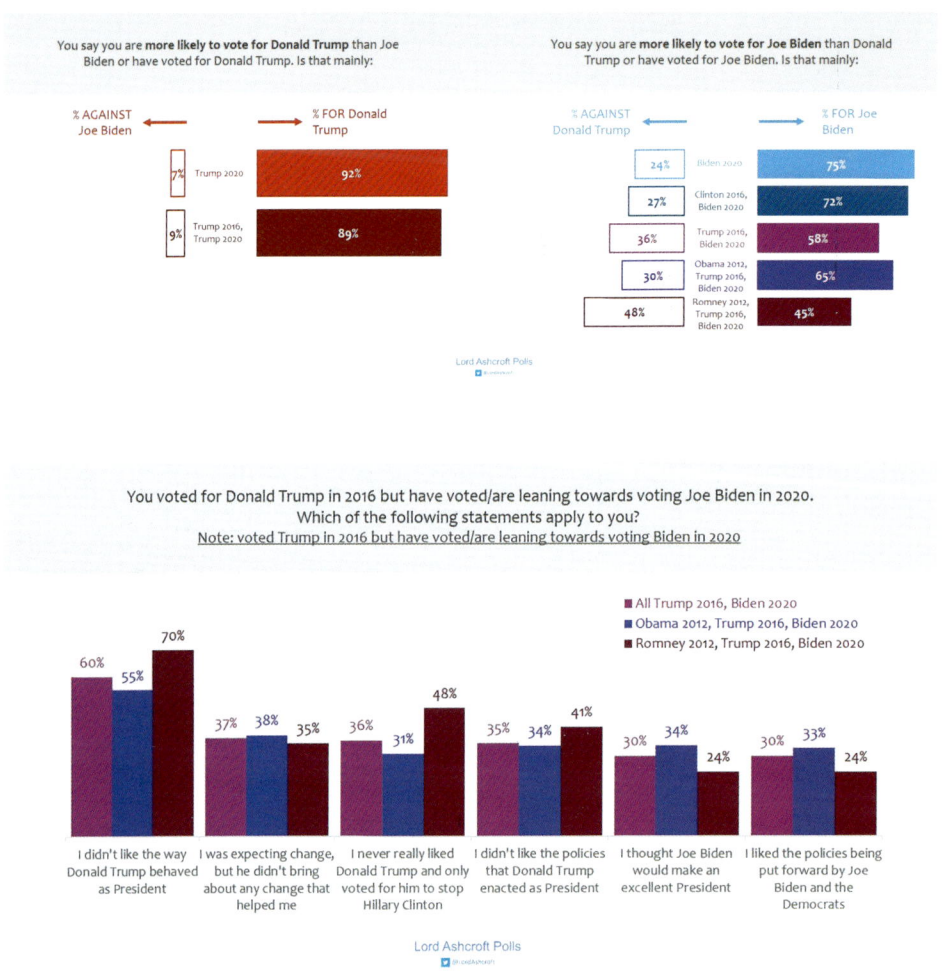

The point was made even more starkly when we asked 2016 Trump voters switching to Biden about their motivations. When we asked if various statements applied to them, by far the most popular was "I didn't like the way Donald Trump behaved as President": six in ten switchers said this had been one of the reasons for their move. This was followed by the complaint that Trump promised change but "didn't bring about any change that helped me"; that they had never really liked Trump in the first place and only voted for him last time to stop Hillary Clinton; and that they didn't like the policies Trump enacted. Two positive statements – "I thought Joe Biden would make an excellent President" and "I liked the policies being put forward by Joe Biden and the Democrats" – were at the very bottom of the list.

What mattered

Even so, those voting for Biden had a clear set of priorities distinct from those of Trump supporters. The Covid pandemic was easily their biggest concern, with 63% of Biden enthusiasts naming it among the top three issues facing the United States today. This was followed by healthcare, chosen by just under half. Race relations was joint third, named as often as the economy and jobs, with the environment and climate change in fourth position.

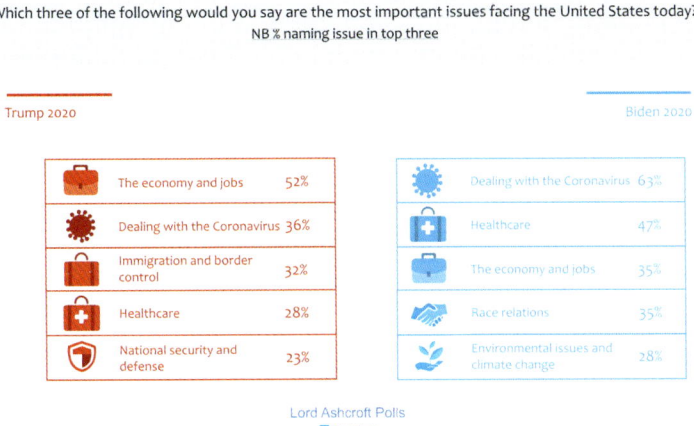

Trump enthusiasts were much more motivated by the economy and jobs, with the pandemic a fairly distant second. Immigration and border control were a bigger issue for them than healthcare.

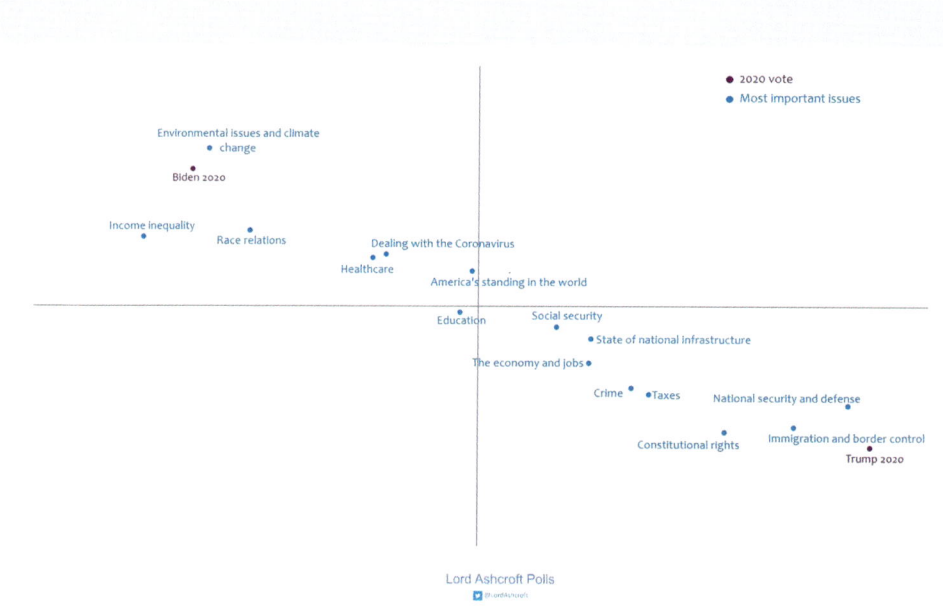

Our political map, created using principal component analysis, shows how different attributes and opinions interact with one another. The closer the plot points are to each other the more closely related they are. In this example, we can see clearly which issues are most closely associated with each candidate. Those for whom the environment and climate change, income inequality, and race relations were among the most important issues were clearly in Biden territory, while those naming constitutional rights, immigration, and national security were closest to the centre of gravity of Trump support.

At least as telling as the differences in their policy concerns was the two sets of voters' relative willingness to put up with the kind of atmosphere that has characterised American politics in recent years. Three quarters of Trump enthusiasts said they would rather have a President "who does the right thing even if it is divisive." But a majority of Biden enthusiasts – including most of those who were switching to the Democrat having voted for Trump in 2016 – said they would prefer a President "who will create a more civil political climate and build consensus, even if I don't agree with everything they do."

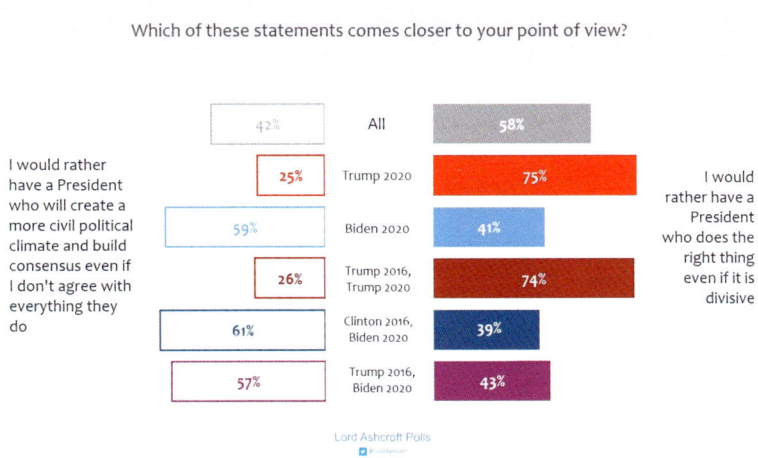

Asked in our focus groups what they hoped or expected to see from a Biden administration, very few of those leaning towards voting for him mentioned specific policies or actions. By far the most common answer was that America under President Biden would be less divided and "more unified." Indeed, they thought this was the main theme of his campaign. "Biden's main pitch is that Trump is mean, and you don't want a mean guy for another four years, do you?", as one Ohio voter put it. The Democrat was saying "a vote for me is just a return to normalcy and some sense of stability and calm." He was "offering some respect and some dignity to the office, an office that we can say we want our kids to look up to, and Donald Trump is not."

The Biden coalition

As with any winning coalition – especially one of this size – the coalition that elected Joe Biden in 2020 brings together a number of disparate elements who do not always see eye to eye. The party's base of committed Democrats has been joined by a group of much more moderate voters who, having backed Trump over Hillary Clinton in 2016, now want to return to a calmer, less acrimonious form of politics; and by a cohort of new voters who did not take part in 2016.

The Democratic base

Democrats did not react well to defeat in 2016. Research I conducted in January 2017 found that those who voted for Hillary Clinton were most likely to blame the election result on people not understanding the issues that were at stake, the media not holding Trump to account, Russian hacking, and fake news. Only around a quarter of Clinton voters blamed a poor campaign, and only one in five said the result had been down to her not being a very good candidate – nearly as many as blamed misogyny or racism.

In focus groups of Michigan Democrats held at the same time, a few said they understood why people had voted for change ("If I were in rural America at the moment, all the industry has been wiped out from overseas competition, I have zero economic options… you bet I'd be pissed"), but they were at least as likely to be disappointed in their fellow electors. Some felt the Trump campaign had had racist undertones; others felt "the bottom line is, they didn't want a woman for President." For most, the problem was that "people just weren't listening" or that voters failed to educate themselves to vote in their own best interests. "I think it was for two reasons," one explained. "'Let's Make America Great Again', and they don't know better."

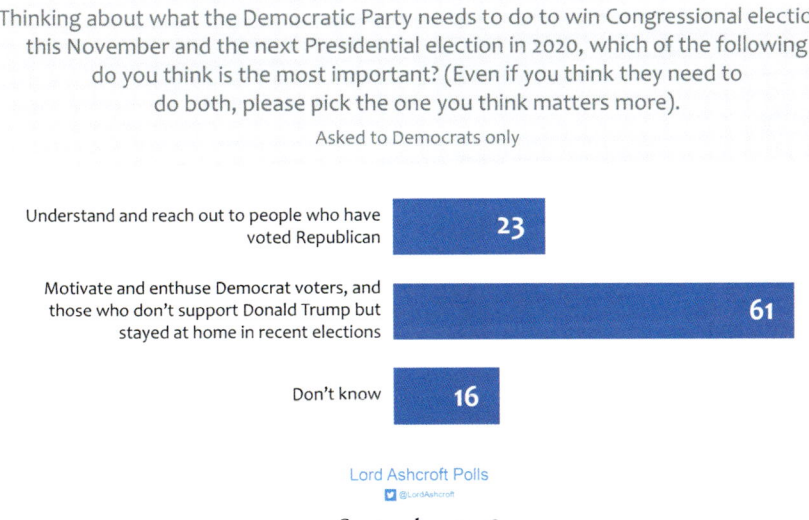

September 2018

Partly as a result of this, I found that Democrats tended to think their path to regaining the White House lay not in convincing Trump voters – who, they felt, were clearly not to be reasoned with – but in enthusing the Democratic base and engaging those who had failed to turn out and vote for Hillary Clinton. In my poll shortly before the midterm elections in 2018, Democrats felt the latter was the priority by 61% to 23%.

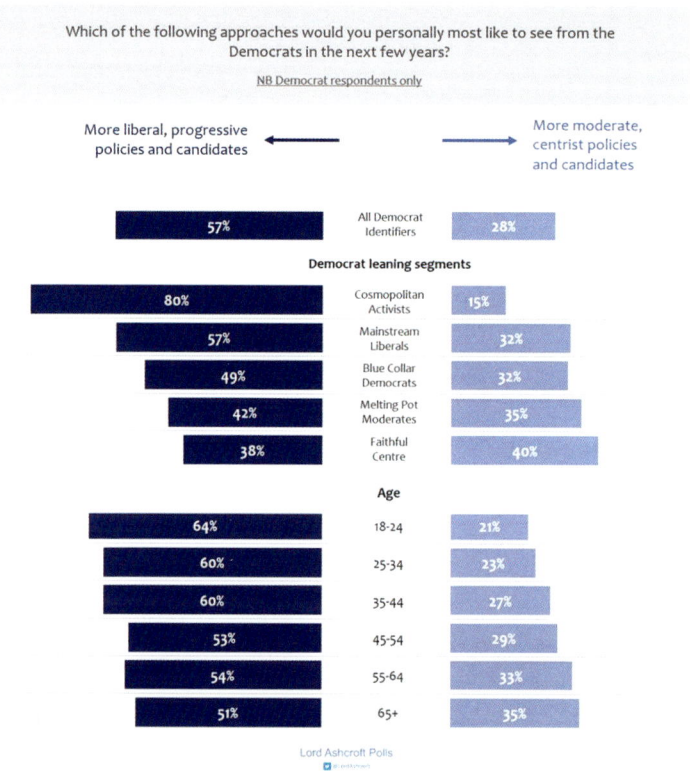

November 2018

Accordingly, few were in the mood to compromise. After the midterms, at the halfway point in the Trump presidency, a majority of Democrats told us they wanted to see the party adopt more liberal, progressive policies and candidates over the next few years, while fewer than three in ten said they would prefer more a more moderate, centrist position. The more politically active and committed to the party they were, the more heavily they leaned to the liberal, progressive option.

The rise of the so-called "Squad" – newly elected US Representatives Alexandria Ocasio-Cortez, Ilhan Omar, Rashida Tlaib and Ayanna Pressley – and the continued popularity in the Democrat ranks of Bernie Sanders and Elizabeth Warren, together with policy proposals such as the Green New Deal, all provided evidence of the party's leftward drift. This was certainly noticed by those outside the party. In focus groups after the midterm elections, otherwise moderate Republicans told us they felt the clash of values was becoming ever starker. "We're no longer Democrat and Republican," one told us, "we are socialism against conservatism. They're not even Democrats anymore. They're really moving towards socialism and it's not Clinton Democrat, it's not John F. Kennedy Democrat, it's scary Democrat."

The entrenchment of positions, and the fading hope of any outreach between parties, was underlined by attitudes to the Mueller investigation into Russian interference in the 2016 election. Nearly nine out of ten Democrats thought Russia acted to try to influence the election, including 78% who thought Donald Trump had been personally aware. Meanwhile, 91% of Republicans believed either that there had been no collusion, or that Russia had not acted at all. We saw the same pattern over the many other accusations against Trump before and during his time in office (or the "witch hunt," as it seemed to his supporters): whether Americans thought he had conspired with Russia, cheated on his taxes, or made illegal campaign payments to an actress depended almost entirely on whether or not they voted for him.

The same was true of whether Americans felt President Trump had committed crimes that warranted his impeachment. As I found shortly before the 2018 midterm elections, nine in ten Trump voters thought there were no such grounds; nine in ten opponents thought the opposite.

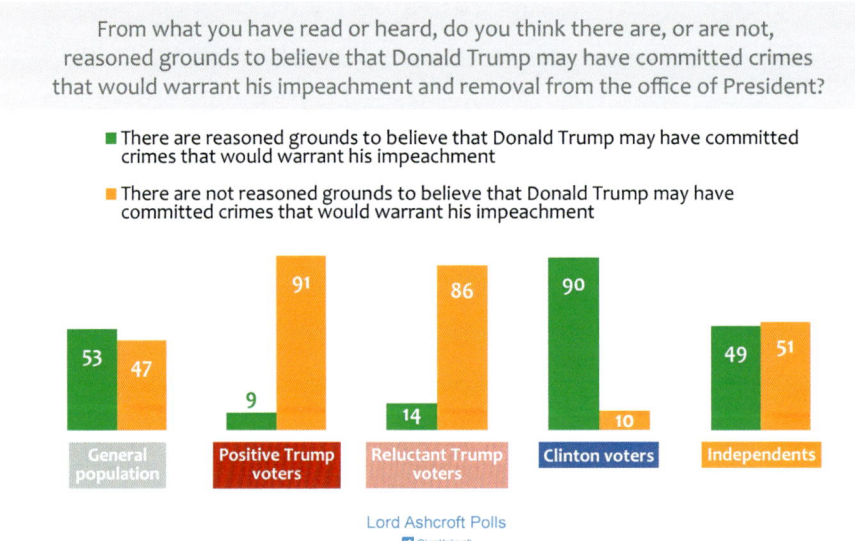

September 2018

As they entered the presidential primary season, Democrats' furious opposition to Trump and their yearning for a more liberal direction came up against the knowledge that their choice of nominee might take them even further from the mainstream voters they would need for victory. In 2016 they had a candidate who alienated too many undecideds without enthusing their own base. But while they knew that the trick was to have it the other way round, many were struggling with the compromise that this was likely to entail, as I found in my research in the fall of 2018 and the spring of 2019.

Many Democrats admired Elizabeth Warren – "an intelligent idealist," as one put it – but there were doubts that she would be able to win the presidency: "She's got as many haters as Hillary." Many remained fond of Bernie Sanders but worried about his age, as well as the limited appeal of his socialist agenda. Moderate and independent voters often thought Joe Biden offered the chance of a welcome return to calm and normality, and many Republicans saw him as the biggest threat to Trump. Many committed Democrats, however, were not yet ready to settle for someone they described to us as "business as usual," "part of the establishment," "too indebted to big corporations," "one of the wealthy crony crowd," and another "rich old white dude."

With a year to go until the general election, there was scant excitement about any of the frontrunners. Though Biden led the field, Democrats in my focus groups told us he seemed to lack new ideas and was showing his age with more "senior moments." Many wondered why, after eight years alongside him in the White House, President Obama had not endorsed him. Sanders still commanded a degree of support among his 2016 fans, but many were now worried about his health and advancing years ("you'd be voting for his VP"), and about the cost of his plans for free college and universal healthcare. This was also a problem for Warren, whom few had warmed to even if she seemed competent; she was described as "shrill," and many found her claims of Native American ancestry bizarre. The candidate most often mentioned positively and spontaneously was "Mayor Pete" Buttigieg, whom they found smart, constructive, impressive and likeable – though some were worried about his relative youth and experience, and whether his "preference," as they often put it, might be a barrier for general election voters: "I'm not sure the country is ready for a gay President with a First Man," as one told us.

Despite these conundrums, a clear divide emerged among Democrats as the proximity of the election began to concentrate minds. In a survey in November 2019, I found that for those who had backed Hillary Clinton over Bernie Sanders in 2016, the single most important factor in choosing a nominee for 2020 was that they should "stand the best chance of beating Donald Trump." For 2016 Sanders voters, this attribute ranked behind having the right priorities for the country, having the right policies to make life better for them and their families, and having values that seemed in tune with their own.

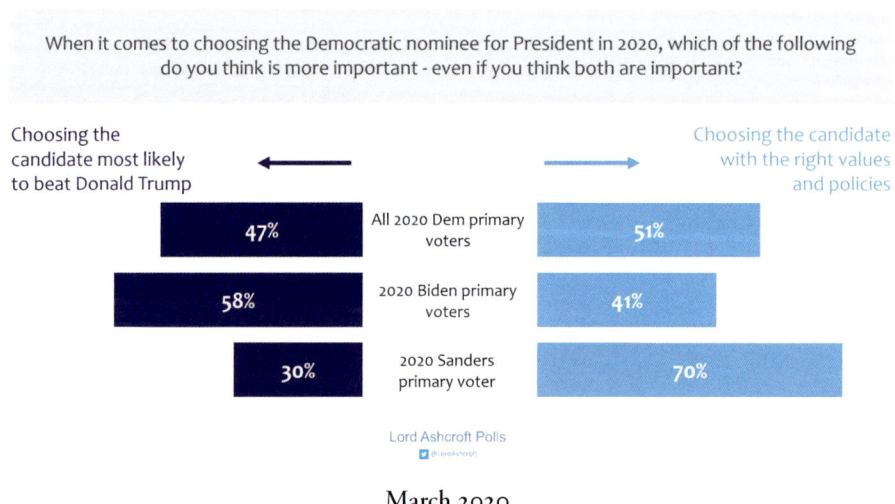

March 2020

In a survey four months later, with the race down to the final two, I gave Democratic primary voters a binary choice between two priorities: "choosing the candidate most likely to beat Donald Trump" or "choosing the candidate with the right values and policies." Beating Trump was the main objective for Biden voters. But by a much bigger margin, those who had supported Sanders said that having the candidate with the right values and priorities mattered more than choosing the one best placed to win in November. Overall, just over two thirds of Americans, including nearly three quarters of Republicans, thought Biden had the better chance of reaching the White House.

In our focus groups at this final stage, very few of the Democrats we spoke to who had voted for Biden in the primary had done so with any enthusiasm. Many told us he had been their second or third choice after their preferred candidate withdrew, or that they had decided he "may be able to pull over some of the centrist Republicans who don't like Trump. It's the best chance to win." Biden was the embodiment of the compromise Democrats knew would be necessary to deny Trump a second term. However uninspiring, it was a compromise most were prepared to make.

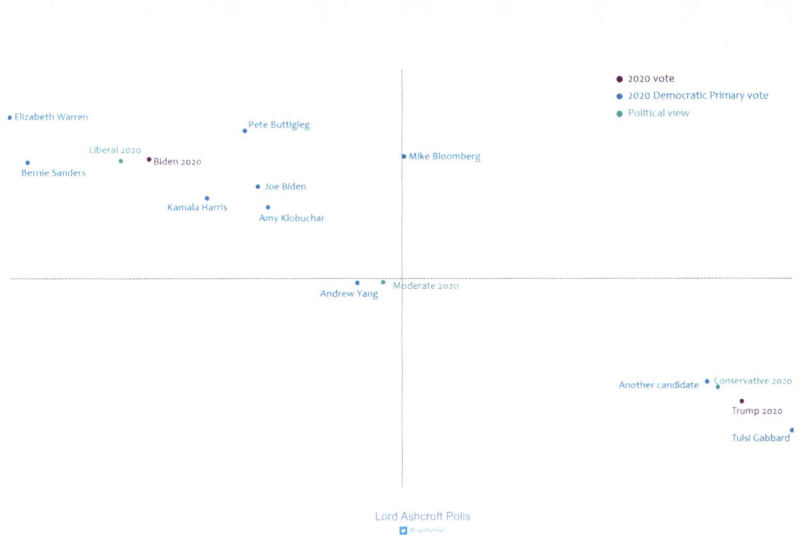

Another of our political maps shows the centre of gravity of support for the main candidates in the 2020 Democratic primary. Warren and Sanders were closest to the epicentre of those who identified as liberal, while Biden, Amy Klobuchar, and especially Andrew Yang found their centre of support much closer to moderate territory. The centre of Biden's general election support is in more liberal territory than his primary support, as more liberal voters took up his cause as the Democratic nominee.

The joiners

Joe Biden, then, was chosen by a largely liberal Democratic base in the hope of attracting the more moderate voters they would need to win the general election. These voters were duly attracted, and, as my survey found, they have some important things in common with their new comrades. Those switching to Biden having voted for Trump in 2016 see the Covid pandemic as the most important issue and the biggest threat facing the country, and they are more worried about healthcare than those who stayed with Trump.

But there are important differences, too. These Trump–Biden switchers are much less likely than Clinton–Biden voters to identify as Democrats, let alone describe themselves as liberal. They are more likely to think of the US as the greatest country in the world – with all that that entails – and much more likely to believe that African Americans and other minorities in America are treated in the same way as white people. They are also more socially and culturally conservative than previous Democrat voters, less keen on gun control and green energy, more wary of big government, and have a less positive view of Democratic icons like Nancy Pelosi, Bernie Sanders, and Elizabeth Warren. They are also less likely to dismiss the previous four years out of hand. Around one third said they approved of the job Trump had done as President, although most of those said they disapproved of his character and personal conduct.

At the same time, the Biden coalition also includes a younger, more ethnically diverse group of people who did not vote in 2016, and who differ in important ways from the former Trump voters who helped elect the new President. They are much more opposed to Trump and all his works and are particularly driven by the view that minorities do not receive equal treatment in the US. They are much less committed to the idea of American exceptionalism, and most of them would rather have a divisive

President who did what they saw as the right thing – while most switchers from Trump want above all to see consensus and calm.

Trump 2016 – Biden 2020, Did not vote 2016 – Biden 2020, Clinton 2016 – Biden 2020

	Trump-Biden	DNV-Biden	Clinton-Biden
Party ID	32% Democrat 37% GOP	59% Democrat	81% Democrat
Politics	13% liberal	38% liberal	49% liberal
Trump presidency	31% approve	4% approve	4% approve
Most important issues	COVID 54% Economy & jobs 43% Healthcare 41%	COVID 60% Healthcare 46% Race relations 39%	COVID 63% Healthcare 47% Economy & jobs 36%
Positive or negative vote?	58% FOR Biden 36% AGAINST Trump	58% FOR Biden 36% AGAINST Trump	72% FOR Biden 27% AGAINST Trump
US exceptionalism	54% America is the greatest country	23% America is the greatest country	32% America is the greatest country
Biggest threats to the US	COVID or another pandemic Economic crisis Government by people with wrong values	COVID or another pandemic Climate change Inequality	COVID or another pandemic Climate change Government by people with wrong values
Biggest fears	Paying for healthcare Immigration policy letting in terrorists Violent crime	Paying for healthcare Unfair treatment by criminal justice system Violent crime	Paying for healthcare Unfair treatment by criminal justice system Violent crime
Minority rights	51% African Americans receive equal treatment	27% African Americans receive equal treatment	30% African Americans receive equal treatment
American dream	68% possible to be successful in America whatever your background	49% possible to be successful in America whatever your background	48% possible to be successful in America whatever your background
Race	70% white	43% white	54% white
Favourability towards (-50/+50):			
Black Lives Matter	👍 +9.21	👍 +27.65	👍 +28.25
National Rifle Association	-0.32	👎 -15.2	👎 -23.58
Republican Party	👎 -5.37	👎 -25.74	👎 -31.79
Democratic Party	👍 +16.34	👍 +23.76	👍 +32.52
Capitalism	👍 +9.2	👎 -6.74	+0.81
Conservatism	👍 +8.22	👎 -12.36	👎 -12.95
Alexandria Ocasio-Cortez	👎 -0.26	👍 +7.79	👍 +15.4

Lord Ashcroft Polls

In the months leading up to the election we held a number of focus groups with African American voters who had supported President Obama in 2012 but not turned out for

Hillary Clinton four years later – an important part of this group of Biden joiners. Many admitted that they had simply not bothered because they thought Clinton was certain to win ("I guess I overestimated the citizens of the United States," as one put it). However, there was also a strong body of opinion that she had simply not deserved their votes. "She was a horrible Senator and Secretary of State," one told us. "The Clintons, back when Bill was in office, incarcerated more black people than anybody. So, you know, a lot of people weren't really feeling the Clintons because of those type of things." As doubtful African American voters in North Carolina had told us before the 2016 election, she seemed "shady" and just wanted "to be the first lady President" and "build a dynasty." They would need a better reason to vote for her than that.

Though some wished in retrospect that they had turned out despite their misgivings ("if I'd known the margin of victory in this state was so small, I definitely would have stopped being so stubborn and just stood in line and voted"), this was not the case for everyone. Many felt, and strongly resented, that the Democrats seemed to take their votes for granted: "She decided that black people were going to vote Democratic, she didn't have to pay attention."

Even so, during the 2020 campaign many said they would turn out this time. "The difference between now and then is that now we have experience," one told us. "Now we see what can happen and what could possibly happen in the future." While the prospect of Trump being re-elected was distressing, it was also real: "His followers are going to come out and vote. So we have to not make the same mistake."

Some of these votes would still be cast only grudgingly, however. "There's no black agenda for the Democrats," one resigned voter told us. "I don't understand why we are so beholden to the Democratic Party. They haven't done anything for the people we are talking about. Once they get into power, they're going to follow their own agenda. How much of that agenda is really going to be about the people and how much is going to be about the self-centred leaders?" Nor were many reassured by the presence of Kamala Harris on the ticket: "She's a token in my opinion. He figured if he can get a black woman behind him, that will bring in the black vote and also a lot of women," one said. Some were also worried about her track record: "As Attorney General in California she locked up more black people than any Republican Attorney General."

Who's calling the shots?

Part of the Biden coalition, then, wanted a quieter, more unifying approach to government, while another part wanted to reverse as much as possible of President Trump's legacy and take the country in a much more liberal or even radical direction. The potential for conflict and disappointment is obvious. The extent to which this comes to pass will depend in part on how the Democrats believe the result came about.

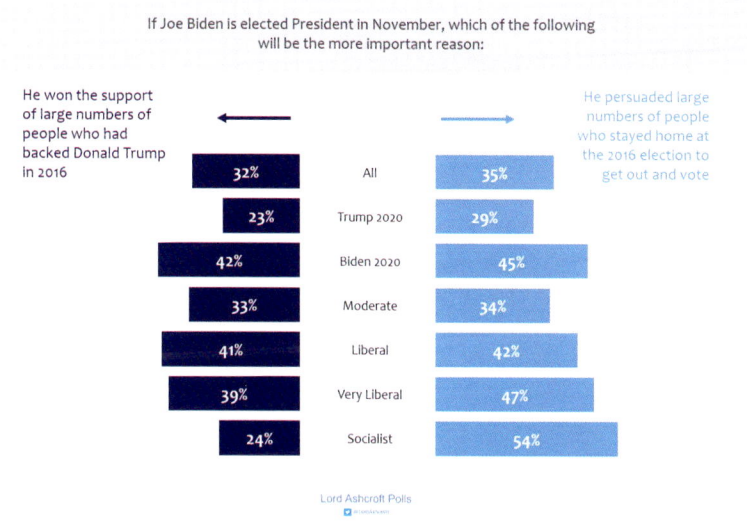

Moderate voters were evenly divided as to whether, if he won, the most important reason would be that Biden persuaded people who stayed at home four years ago to get out and vote, or whether he would have converted large numbers of 2016 Trump voters. However, they were also the least likely to have a view one way or the other. The more liberal or left-wing, the more likely people were to think the key had been mobilising previous non-voters, rather than winning over 2016 Trump supporters – and the less likely, it follows, to think that moderate former Trump voters were an important part of their coalition who need to be accommodated.

Even on the Republican side, few doubted that Joe Biden himself was on the moderate side of the Democratic movement – our focus groups regularly described him as "mild," "middle-of-the-road," "laid back," and "the safe pick." However, many felt he now represented a minority in his party, which had chosen him as the most electable candidate to front what would turn out to be a much more radical agenda. "It's more and more obvious that the whole point of the left is to get him into office, and then I think his role is going to diminish, and others in the party who are a lot more liberal with their agendas are going to be running things. Biden was the obvious pick to be moderate and just vanilla… He's the path of least resistance for the far left," as one put it. "I think Joe wants to be a moderate," said another. "But he has to agree with people that are so far left that he says one thing and really means another." Some were worried that Biden was "a kind of puppet for Nancy Pelosi and everyone else behind them. He's pretty old. I don't see him really standing up for anything except what the Democrats want him to say." There were concerns about "the whole Squad – AOC and Kamala and Bernie Sanders."

More specifically, they worried that his age and (to them) evident infirmity would mean he would serve one term at most – clearing the way for Kamala Harris, whom they regarded as a much less moderate force. "If you watch his speeches, he's cognitively not all there. He's just not," was a typical observation. "At the debate he just faded out at the end like he wanted to go to bed." One described Biden as "the transition-in-chief." After the election they would "take him to a doctor and give him a test and say, 'Oh, he's deemed incompetent. Here's our new President." The Speaker had "already reminded us of the Twenty-Fifth Amendment so she can remove his ass and Kamala will be President."

While some wavering voters feared that Biden would be a transition to a more liberal agenda, some on the Democrat side hoped this would be the case. "I kind of like Kamala and, I mean, he'll be 78 years old, so I like my chances of getting her in there," said one. Another saw Biden as a necessary pause before the government could take a more radical direction: "Let's get some distance from the Trump administration, reset a little bit, and then in the next election let's hope someone can come in and lead, like AOC."

A reunited nation?

ONE OF THE BIGGEST hopes for Joe Biden supporters is that a new President would be able to put an end to the discord that has characterised American politics for many years and usher in a new, less rancorous era. Though it has become a cliché to talk about the polarisation that dominates today's politics, the problem is not that people disagree, as they always have. The difference is that rather than trying to mediate those divisions, politics has emphasised and supercharged them.

This has been the case for over two decades: President Clinton's failed healthcare reforms, the 1994 Republican Revolution, the Clinton impeachment, the hanging chads of the Bush–Gore election, the Iraq War, the financial crisis, Obamacare and the rise of the Tea Party all combined with the rise of talk radio, cable news, and social media to create the political atmosphere that existed before the man who became the 45th President announced his candidacy. What, then, are these divisions, and what are the prospects of President Biden putting an end to them?

Two tribes

A side-by-side comparison of Trump and Biden enthusiasts reveals deep and genuine differences between the two in outlook, political priorities, and demographic characteristics. As we saw in the previous chapter, the economy and jobs were the most important issues facing the country, but only fourth on the list for Biden enthusiasts, for whom Covid easily topped the agenda. Immigration and border control appeared in the top four for enthusiasts of Trump but not Biden; the reverse was true for healthcare and race relations.

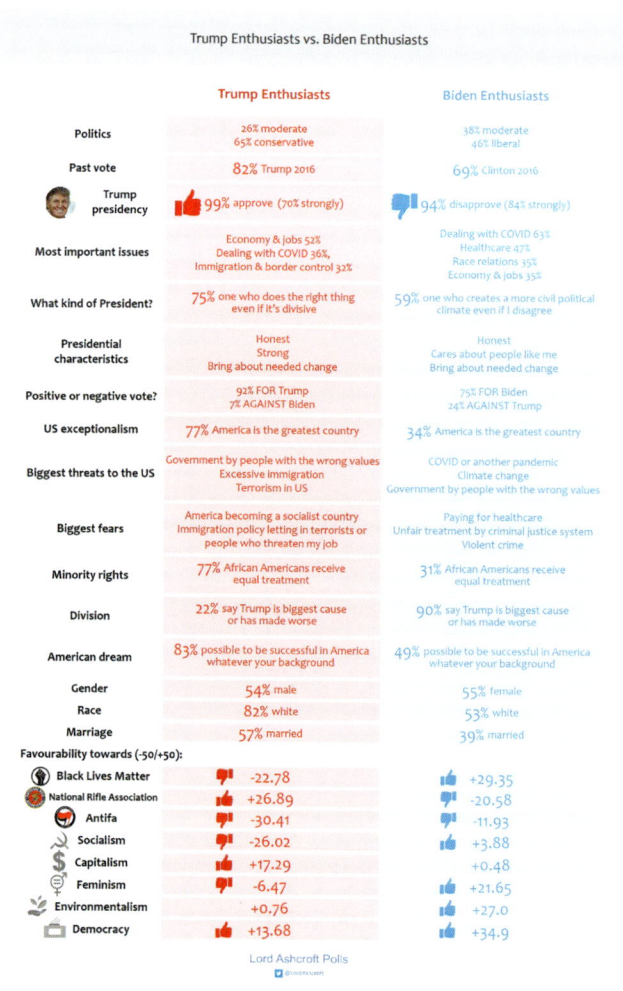

The gulf between how Trump and Biden enthusiasts felt about Black Lives Matter was nearly as great as was the difference in their opinions of the National Rifle Association. The two sets of voters also had diametrically opposed views on whether it was more important to control gun ownership or to protect the right of Americans to bear arms. The different favourability scores the two groups gave for capitalism, socialism, feminism, and environmentalism were also instructive, as was the less positive score Trump enthusiasts gave for democracy itself – which perhaps reflects greater dissatisfaction with the political process as currently practised in Washington.

Accordingly, there were also huge differences in how the two sets of voters viewed life in America. For example, more than three quarters of Trump enthusiasts agreed with the statement "African Americans and other minorities have the same rights and are treated in the same way in the United States as whites"; in the Biden camp, only three in ten concurred. An overwhelming majority of Trump supporters believed that "if you work hard, it is possible to be very successful in America no matter what your background," a view shared by fewer than half of Biden enthusiasts.

Fears and threats

Further sharp differences were revealed, and indeed explained, when we asked voters how afraid they were of various scenarios. For Biden enthusiasts, the biggest fears were being unable to pay for healthcare if they or a family member became seriously ill, unfair treatment by the criminal justice system, and violent crime. Trump enthusiasts were more worried about America becoming a socialist country like those in Europe, and immigration policies letting in terrorists and people who threaten their job.

A reunited nation?

On a scale of 0 (not afraid at all) to 100 (very afraid) please say how afraid you are that the following things may happen?
NB, mean score

All

Not being able to pay for my health insurance or healthcare if I, or a member of my family, becomes seriously ill	62
A member of my family or friends being the victim of a violent crime	60
Losing my job or source of income	57

Trump 2020

America becoming a socialist country like those in Europe	73
Immigration policies allowing terrorists into the United States who threaten my community	72
Immigration policies allowing people into the United States who threaten my job	60

Biden 2020

Not being able to pay for my health insurance or healthcare if I, or a member of my family, becomes seriously ill	67
A member of my family or friends being treated unfairly by the criminal justice system	62
A member of my family or friends being the victim of a violent crime	62

Trump 2016, Trump 2020

America becoming a socialist country like those in Europe	73
Immigration policies allowing terrorists into the United States who threaten my community	72
Immigration policies allowing people into the United States who threaten my job	59

Clinton 2016, Biden 2020

Not being able to pay for my health insurance or healthcare if I, or a member of my family, becomes seriously ill	65
A member of my family or friends being treated unfairly by the criminal justice system	60
A member of my family or friends being the victim of a violent crime	59

Trump 2016, Biden 2020

Not being able to pay for my health insurance or healthcare if I, or a member of my family, becomes seriously ill	62
Immigration policies allowing terrorists into the United States who threaten my community	61
A member of my family or friends being the victim of a violent crime	60

Non-Hispanic White

Not being able to pay for my health insurance or healthcare if I, or a member of my family, becomes seriously ill	59
Immigration policies allowing terrorists into the United States who threaten my community	58
A member of my family or friends being the victim of a violent crime	56

Black or African American

A member of my family or friends being treated unfairly by the criminal justice system	74
A member of my family or friends being killed by a police officer in my community	71
A member of my family or friends being the victim of a violent crime	68

Hispanic, Latino or Spanish

Not being able to pay for my health insurance or healthcare if I, or a member of my family, becomes seriously ill	70
Losing my job or source of income	69
A member of my family or friends being the victim of a violent crime	68

Lord Ashcroft Polls
@LordAshcroft

There were also sharp differences according to race. While white voters as a whole were most worried about paying for healthcare, immigration policy, and crime, African Americans – whose scores indicated that they were at least as worried about healthcare and crime as white voters – were even more worried about the prospect of a friend or family member being treated unfairly by the criminal justice system or killed by a police officer in their community. The biggest worries for Hispanic voters were paying for healthcare, losing their job, and violent crime.

Differences also emerged when we asked how the two camps assessed various threats to America. Of the nine items we put forward, the least serious for Trump enthusiasts was climate change, which ranked second for Biden enthusiasts after Covid or a similar pandemic in the future. Excessive immigration, meanwhile, received the lowest threat rating from Biden supporters but came second on the Trump enthusiasts' list.

How serious a threat is each of the following to America today, where 0 means it is not a threat at all and 100 means it is an extremely serious threat?

[NB Mean score]

	All		Trump 2020		Biden 2020	
1	People with the wrong values and priorities having control of our government	78	People with the wrong values and priorities having control of our government	78	Covid-19 or a similar pandemic in the future	86
2	Covid-19 or a similar pandemic in the future	76	Excessive immigration	75	Climate change	82
3	The risk of a new economic and financial crisis	74	Terrorism within the United States	72	People with the wrong values and priorities having control of our government	81
4	Division and polarisation in American society	73	The risk of a new economic and financial crisis	69	Inequality in American society	80
5	Inequality in American society	68	Division and polarisation in American society	69	Division and polarisation in American society	79
6	Terrorism within the United States	68	Covid-19 or a similar pandemic in the future	67	The risk of a new economic and financial crisis	78
7	Climate change	68	Military conflict with another country	59	Terrorism within the United States	70
8	Military conflict with another country	61	Inequality in American society	55	Military conflict with another country	63
9	Excessive immigration	57	Climate change	52	Excessive immigration	46

Lord Ashcroft Polls

With the exception of excessive immigration and domestic terrorism, Biden enthusiasts' threat scores suggested that they were more worried about every scenario than their Trumpian counterparts. The difference was particularly stark when it came to climate change (52/100 for Trump enthusiasts, 82 for Biden enthusiasts), inequality in American society (55 and 80) and Covid or a similar pandemic in the future (67 and 86).

However, the two groups tellingly both regarded "people with the wrong values and priorities having control of our government" as a very serious threat indeed. Trump enthusiasts put it at the top of their list with a score of 78/100; Biden enthusiasts ranked it third, though with an even higher score of 81.

Values

Looking in more detail at those values, we see sharply divergent views on practically all the issues of principle that permeate political debate in America, including the role of government, how the Supreme Court should interpret the Constitution, the place of religion in national life, abortion, the availability of welfare benefits, and – especially – gun ownership rights. Notably, 2016 Trump voters switching to Biden tend to come down on the same side of each question as longer-standing Democrat voters, but by a much narrower margin.

Where did you hear that?

Different voting groups differed not just in what they thought about politics, but where they got their information about it. Those for whom MSNBC is their most watched TV news channel or for whom Twitter or a national newspaper are the main sources

A reunited nation?   37

of political news are most likely to be found very close to the centre of support for Joe Biden. In the opposite corner, those most likely to have supported Donald Trump in 2020 are very close to those whose main news sources are talk radio or Fox News.

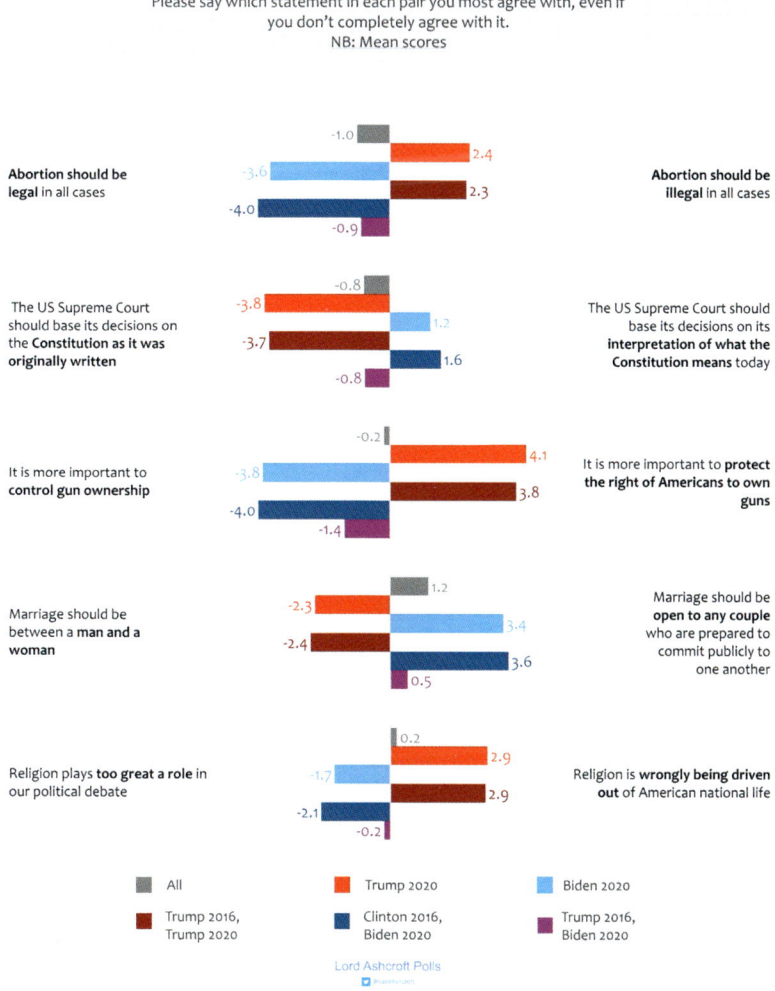

A reunited nation?

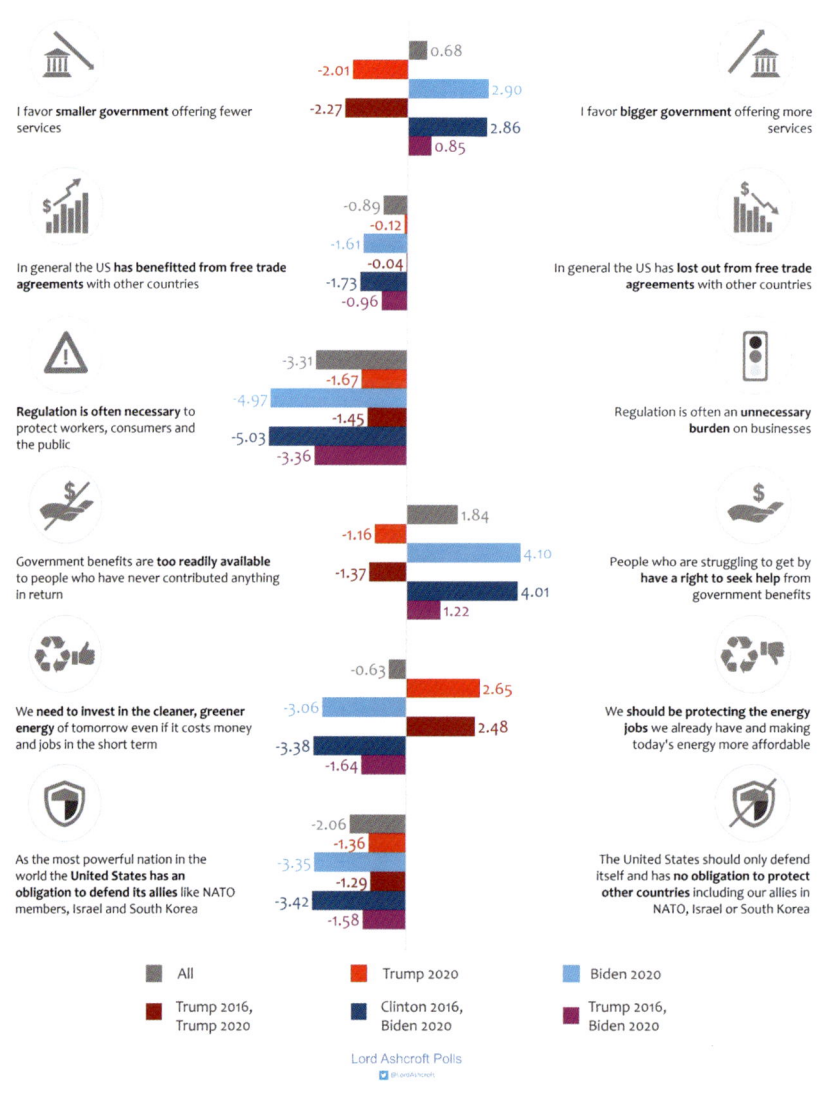

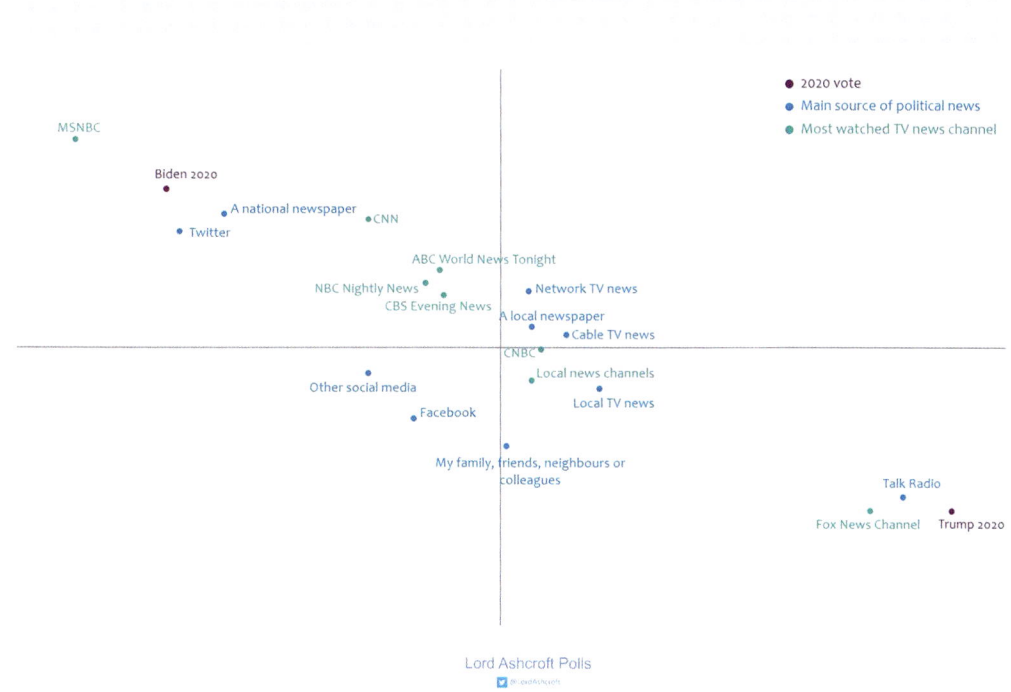

Minority rights

As we have seen, the question of whether African Americans and other minorities have the same rights and are treated in the same way as white people was a particularly animating one, especially for voters who became enthusiasts for Joe Biden. In our poll, we found voters as a whole slightly more likely to agree than disagree that minorities do in fact receive equal treatment in the US. Despite the racially charged controversies of the last four years, this shows almost no change since our pre-election survey in 2016 when 50% agreed with the statement, strongly or otherwise, and 44% did not.

A reunited nation?

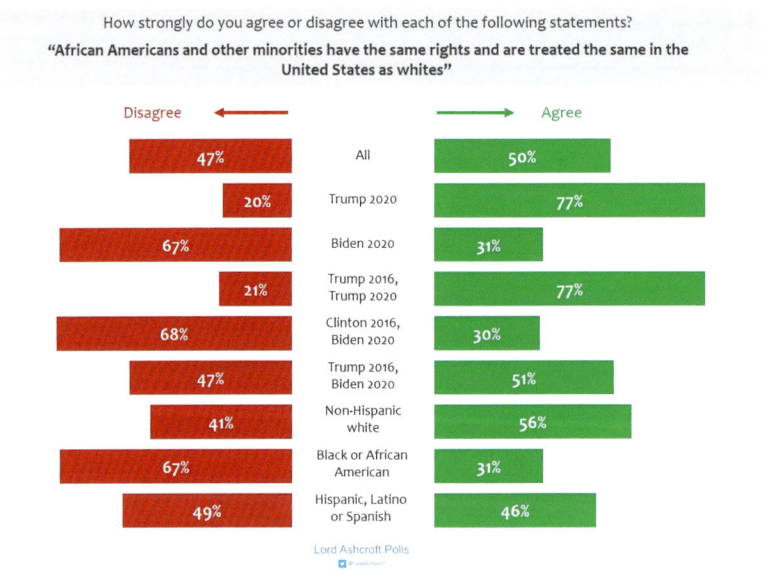

There was also little change within racial groups themselves. Agreement among white voters rose from 55% to 56%, remained exactly the same at 46% among Hispanic or Latino voters, and actually increased from 25% to 31% among African Americans.

Among Democrats, however, agreement that minorities have the same rights and are treated in the same way as white Americans fell from 39% to 34% (and 31% of Biden enthusiasts) and rose dramatically among Republicans from 61% to 73% (and 77% of Trump enthusiasts). Previous Trump voters now leaning to Biden agreed with the statement by a similar narrow margin to that of voters as a whole.

Strikingly, Biden enthusiasts were more likely to agree with the statement "Donald Trump is a racist" (93%) than were African Americans (82%) or Hispanic voters (71%). It is also notable, however, that while 85% of Trump enthusiasts rejected the statement, 12% of them agreed with it.

A reunited nation?

Early in his presidency, African American voters in our focus groups debated whether Trump himself was a racist or was simply playing up to what they saw as racist tendencies within his electoral base. "I think he stirs the pot, and once he stirs the pot and it's boiling over, he's like, 'Ah, well… On to the next thing. How 'bout that NFL taking a knee?'" Either way, they felt his language and tone were having an impact on their lives. Some spoke from experience. "Where I work, I can tell now from maybe a year ago, the way people interact with me, and they look at me different," a Hispanic voter in Las Vegas told us. "I had a guest call me a 'boy', and I've been working at my hotel for seven years. Even my director, he said, 'Oh, can you tell that black boy to…' And I'm not even black." During the 2020 campaign, one woman said, "he's bringing out the racists that for many years were calm in this country. Now, when he talks, all those racist people say, 'All right, this is my time.' I'm 40, and this is the first time in my life living in this country that I feel worried about my safety."

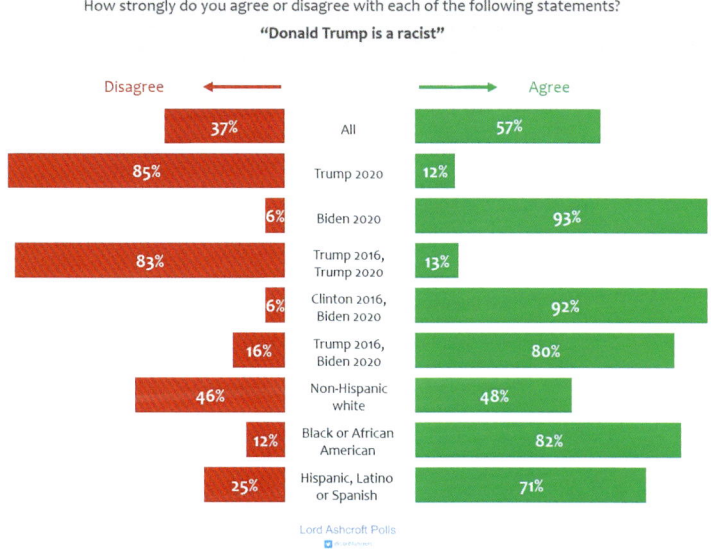

For his opponents, it followed that Trump supporters, if not actually racists themselves, must at least have quite a high tolerance for racism to be prepared to vote for him. That being the case, the problem was not going to go away. "Biden is not going to cure racism," we were told. "We already know we're surrounded by it. All these people voted for Trump, and we're living among them."

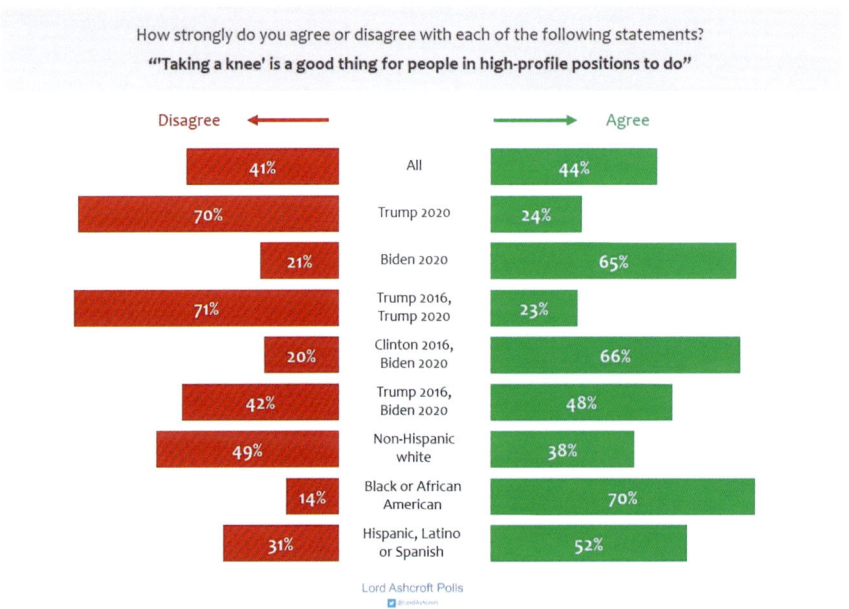

The two sets of voters had very different views on taking a knee, a gesture of which President Trump had been fiercely critical since it was initiated by San Francisco 49ers quarterback Colin Kaepernick in 2016. I found Americans as a whole quite evenly divided on the question. Forty-four per cent said they thought it was a good thing for people in high-profile positions to do, including two thirds of Biden enthusiasts and 70% of African Americans, but only just over half of Hispanics and 38% of white voters. Trump–Biden switchers were less keen than Biden supporters as a whole, supporting the gesture from public figures by 48% to 42%. Seven in ten Trump enthusiasts disagreed that taking a knee was a good thing for high-profile people to do, as did 41% of the population in general.

A number of African Americans in our focus groups also had doubts about the gesture. "It's a game at the end of the day," said one. "Sure, it does show some solidarity with us because obviously the Trump administration is completely against it. But do I believe that when Joe or even, heck, Nancy Pelosi got down on one knee it was a heartfelt message? No."

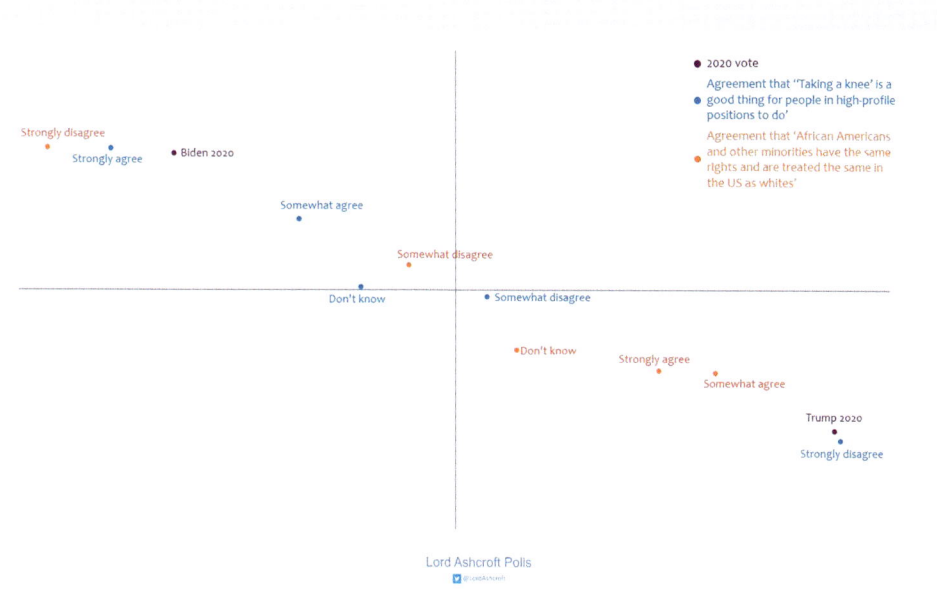

44 A reunited nation?

This map shows how closely people's attitudes to these questions are related to their position in the general election. Those who disagree strongly that minorities receive equal treatment in the US and agree that taking a knee is a good thing for public figures to do are close to the centre of gravity of support for Biden. The epicentre of Trump support, meanwhile, is close to those who believe minorities do receive equal treatment and – especially – disapprove of high-profile figures taking a knee.

Attitudes mapped

Combining these various views and attributes on one map makes for an interesting picture of the electorate. Again, we see here how different issues, attributes, personalities and opinions interact with one another. The closer the plot points are to each other the more closely related they are.

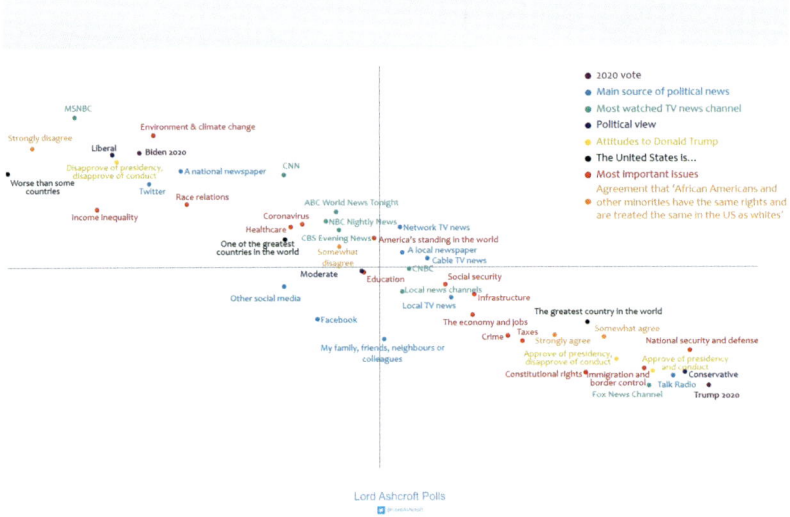

We can therefore see how issue concerns, political outlook, news sources and views of American life and Donald Trump's presidency were associated with support with one or another candidate at the 2020 election.

Does it matter who wins?

Given that both sets of voters regard government by people with the wrong values and priorities as one of the biggest threats facing the country, it is not surprising that – in another rare point of agreement – identically high proportions of Trump and Biden enthusiasts agreed that "whether Donald Trump or Joe Biden is the President will have a big impact on America." Fewer than one in five Americans overall thought "it doesn't matter who wins the election, America will be the same" – though it is notable that African Americans were considerably more likely to take this view (26%) than white voters (16%).

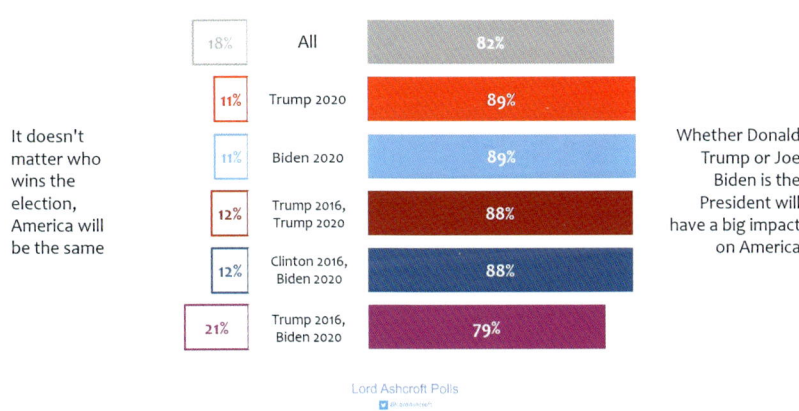

This sentiment was echoed in our pre-election focus groups, on both sides. As we saw in the previous chapter, the concern many voters had about Biden was not his personal platform but the much more radical agenda that might come to the fore if he were elected, and especially if his age and health compelled him to step aside for Kamala Harris. "It could be our whole way of life that's at stake," said one worried Republican. It's not just a few Democratic ideas, it's upheaval of the whole system. The Green New Deal: he wants to get rid of oil. It doesn't make sense, it's just something that sound good when a bunch of Berkeley students are arguing." Another said, "At previous elections I've felt that if my guy doesn't win, things are going to be OK. This isn't one of those elections." On the other side, an African American supporter of Joe Biden said it was "traumatic" to think Trump might be President again.

Bad, or just wrong?

These divisions are not just a matter of different people with opposing views about politics, but the way each side views the motivations of the other. On this question, we see people on the right taking a slightly more generous view of their opponents than those on the left.

Two thirds of Republicans said they thought people who vote Democrat and support Joe Biden were "good people who want good things for America, we just disagree about how to achieve them." However, only just over half of Democrats were prepared to say the same about Republicans and Trump voters: 42% said these were "bad people who want the wrong things for America," including majorities of those who voted for Bernie Sanders in the 2020 primaries and those who describe themselves as very liberal, and two thirds of self-declared socialists.

A reunited nation?

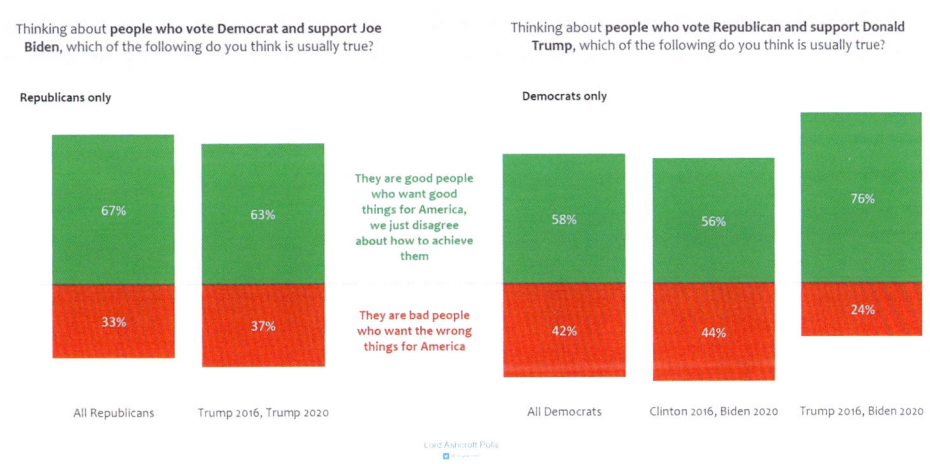

Trump the divider, Biden the uniter?

Nine out of ten Biden enthusiasts said either that they thought Donald Trump was the biggest cause of recent divisions in society (54%) or that he had made existing divisions worse (36%). Switchers from Trump to Biden agreed, though they were more likely to say Trump had exacerbated divisions than created them.

Notably, African American and Hispanic respondents were less likely than Biden enthusiasts to think Trump was the biggest cause of division, and considerably more likely to say the country would be just as divided had he never entered politics.

While Republicans in our focus groups felt and regretted that the country was divided, most did not feel this had very much to do with Trump. "Why are people saying Trump is the one dividing the country? The people that are in conflict are in conflict because of their belief systems and what they think is important." After all, "we've had conflict well before this, with Trayvon Martin, and that was all with Obama. So just because we have a new President doesn't mean the conflict is going to end." There were also "paid agitators like Antifa, and it's in their best interests to keep everything in chaos to accomplish whatever their agenda is."

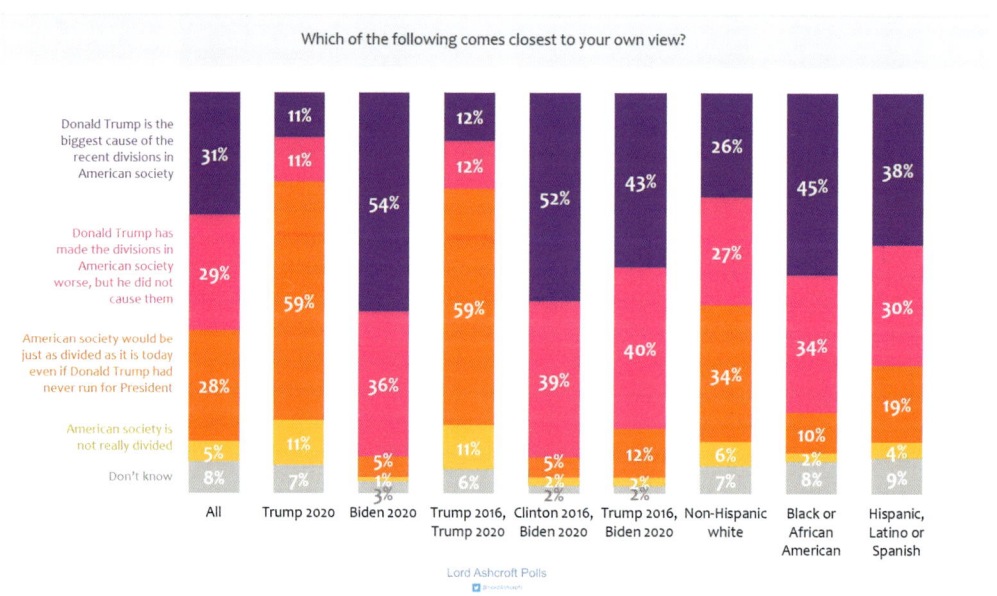

Accordingly, the two camps took different views when asked about politics in the post-Trump era. Only a small minority of voters thought things would "go back to normal quite quickly" when Trump left office. But while a majority of Biden enthusiasts and almost half of Biden–Trump switchers thought things would gradually return to normal, six in ten Trump enthusiasts thought politics would either remain just as divisive (36%) or become even more divisive (24%) after Trump's eventual departure. African American voters (55%) were more likely than voters as a whole (44%) to think politics would quickly or gradually return to normal after Trump left office.

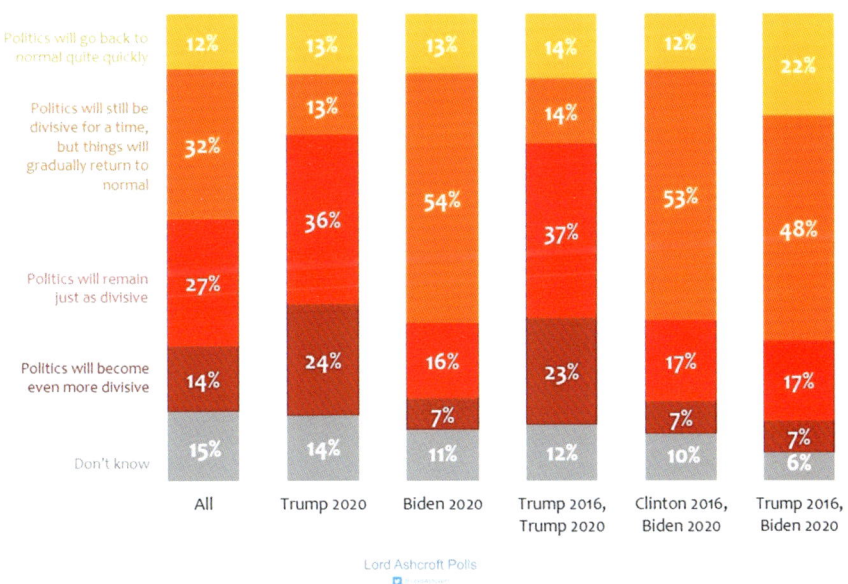

While Biden supporters often said they wanted more unity and less division, this often seemed less evident in the way they spoke about the people who voted for Trump. "There's a lot of effing stupid people in our country," said one Democrat reflecting on the 2016 result. "Idiots and frickin' old, racist white men." The idea that his voters had simply lacked guidance by better informed people such as themselves was also a regular theme: "Did we not do enough to reach out? Did we not do enough educating the people in our lives?" agonised one woman. "Some of my friends have Trump signs all over their yard and I still love them, and our children still play together. But that doesn't mean I don't think they have received stupid misinformation."

Trump voters were all too aware of how Democrats saw them. Hillary Clinton's description of a "basket of deplorables" was firmly fixed in their memory as the authentic expression of what liberals really thought. "She was talking about us," one Republican told us three years after Clinton had uttered the phrase. "I think she was talking about the working-class people." In doing so "she showed me she wasn't interested in understanding my perspective whatsoever." Democrats "preach compassion and understanding, but only if you agree with them."

Some Republicans therefore felt strongly that the calls for agreement and consensus were only really aimed in one direction. "I'm a middle-aged white conservative Christian male. All of this inclusiveness and unity, and what they're really saying is that nobody else has to change their mindset but me." The supposedly tolerant left "is only tolerant if you agree with their opinion. If you voted for Trump, then you're the enemy."

As for the idea of Biden ending the divisions, "it's like they're going to wave a magic wand and fix everything that's wrong now. If Jesus came back and was the President, I'm not sure he himself could do it." Whoever the President is, "you can't tell everyone to get along or make a law that says everybody gets along. You have to model good behaviour and hope for the best."

The new American electorate – where they ended up

My research at the 2016 election identified ten distinct segments of voters within the overall electorate. These were based on detailed analysis of our polling not just on people's political views but on questions including background, ethnicity, family, housing, education, health, work, income, interest in current affairs, religion, political commitment, news sources, their attitudes to big questions, and their level of contentment with life.

A reunited nation?

Four years later, we recreated these groups from our poll during the campaign to see how far they had moved politically, and in which direction, comparing their recalled 2016 vote with the candidate they said they were most likely to support in our October 2020 survey. Overall, we see a general swing to the Democrats, but with both poles moving even further towards their own party.

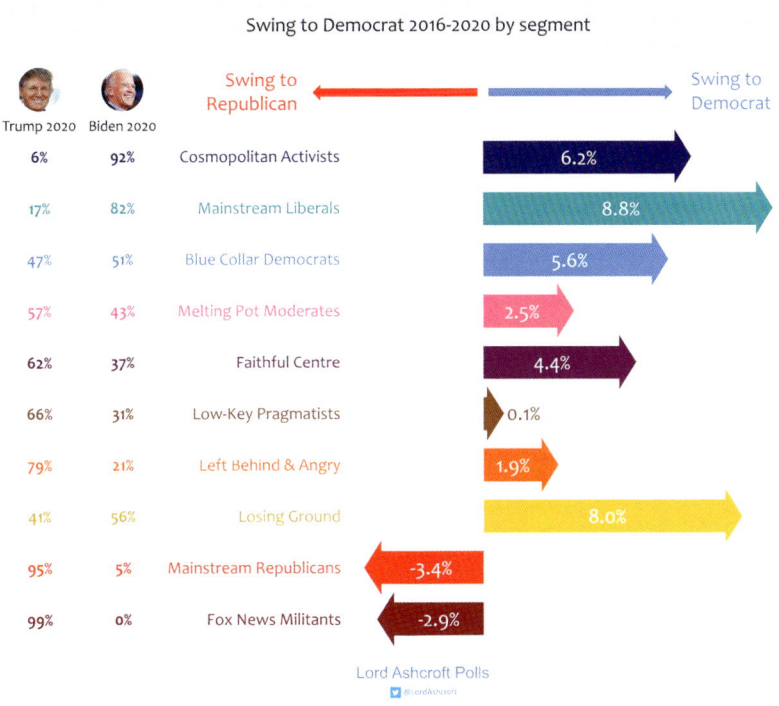

Cosmopolitan Activists were the most active in politics, and more likely to share political information on social media, attend rallies, and donate to political campaigns than any other segment. Disproportionately younger, female, and in full-time education, they were the most likely of all the segments to possess a valid US passport. They were more likely than most to name CNN or MSNBC as their main news source, and three quarters described themselves as liberal or progressive. They were the most likely to have a positive view of government regulation and benefits, gun control, investment in green energy, same-sex marriage, immigration, multiculturalism, social liberalism and feminism, and to think religion plays too great a role in political debate. They were also the most likely to think globalisation had been a force for good and that the US had benefited from free trade deals with other countries.

Biden 92%, Trump 6%. 6% swing to Democrat since 2016.

Mainstream Liberals tended to be younger, female, and highly educated, though racially similar to the US as a whole. Mostly liberals or moderates, they had an average interest in politics with local outlets, CNN, and MSNBC their most important sources of news. They thought that religion played too great a role in political debate and took an interpretive approach to the Constitution. An overwhelming majority favoured gun control, and they were among the most likely to think of immigration and feminism as forces for good. They tended to be pro-choice, overwhelmingly supported same-sex marriage, and were more likely than most to think the US had benefited from free trade deals, take a positive view of government regulation, and favour investment in green energy.

Biden 82%, Trump 17%. 9% swing to Democrat since 2016.

Blue Collar Democrats were the most likely to remain living in the town where they grew up, and tended to be younger, with a below average level of education. Half were non-white, one quarter Hispanic, and half had children under eighteen, making them the group most likely to do so. More likely than most to attend church regularly, three quarters believed that religion was wrongly being driven out of American national life; one third identified as Catholics. They tended to be pro-life, and overwhelmingly supported same-sex marriage. They were also among the most likely to see immigration as a force for good. They were much more supportive of gun ownership rights than other parts of the Democratic Core. They favoured the idea of bigger government offering more services and were among the least likely to think government benefits are too readily available. Though they believed in climate change, they thought protecting jobs and making today's energy more affordable were more important than investing in green energy for the future.

Biden 51%, Trump 47%. 6% swing to Democrat since 2016.

Melting Pot Moderates

Among the most likely to have been born outside the US, nearly half the segment was non-white. Most saw immigration and multiculturalism as mixed blessings, and they were more likely than most to be neutral or evenly divided on other questions, including gun control, the benefit of trade agreements, and US intervention abroad. Nearly half described themselves as moderate. They were positive about life in the US, and among the most likely to think people who work hard can be successful in America whatever their background. Most saw more opportunities than threats from the way economy and society are changing.

Trump 57%, Biden 43%. 3% swing to Democrat since 2016.

Faithful Centre

Half described themselves as evangelical or born-again Christians, and three quarters thought religion was being wrongly driven out of American national life. Two thirds described themselves as moderate or conservative. Members of this segment were the most likely of all to have been born outside the US; half were non-white, and a quarter African American. They were divided on the benefits of immigration, gun control, and trade agreements and tended to be pro-life. They were more likely than most to see feminism and social liberalism as mixed blessings, but also to think that for most children growing up in America life would be better than it was for their parents.

Trump 62%, Biden 37%. 4% swing to Democrat since 2016.

Low-Key Pragmatists

Predominantly white and female, most described themselves as moderate or conservative. They had a below average level of church attendance, supported same-sex marriage and were marginally pro-choice. Two thirds considered life in America worse than it was thirty years ago, and they were more likely than most to think life would be worse for most children growing up in America today than it was for their parents. They were more likely than average to think immigration had been a force for ill, tended to support gun ownership rights, were sceptical of bigger government, and thought the US had lost out from free trade agreements.

Trump 66%, Biden 31%. No swing since 2016.

Left Behind & Angry

Predominantly white, older, and less likely than average to have a college education, more than half described themselves as conservative or very conservative. Their church attendance was higher than average and they thought religion was wrongly being driven out of American national life. Most thought life would be worse for most American children than it was for their parents, that life in the US was worse overall than it was thirty years ago, and that changes in society and the economy were bringing more threats than opportunities. They were the most likely to think immigration had been a force for ill, tended to think the US had lost out from free trade deals, and were less likely than most to think America had a responsibility to defend its NATO allies.

Trump 79%, Biden 21%. 2% swing to Democrat since 2016.

Losing Ground

Less likely than average to have a college education, these were the most likely to be unemployed. Most described themselves as moderate or conservative, though they were less likely than most to take an interest in politics. They were on the fence on some controversial issues but were more likely than most to see immigration as a mixed blessing or a force for ill. They were among the most likely to think life in America was worse overall than it was thirty years ago, that changes in society were bringing more threats than opportunities, that life for most children growing up in America would be worse than it was for their parents, and that people from some backgrounds would never have a real chance to be successful no matter how hard they worked.

Biden 56%, Trump 41%. 8% swing to Democrat since 2016.

Republican Mainstream

Disproportionately male, married, older, and white, half described themselves as conservative and a further quarter as moderate. They were more likely than most to have shared political information on social media, put up yard signs, and contributed to political campaigns. One third described themselves as born-again or evangelical Christians, and most thought religion was wrongly being driven out of American national life. They tended to be pro-life and were more likely than most segments to be opposed to same-sex marriage, or neutral. They were the most likely to say that people who work hard can be successful in America whatever their background, but also more likely than most to think that for most children growing up in America today life would be worse than it was for their parents, that changes in the economy and society were bringing more threats than opportunities, and that life in America was worse overall than it was thirty years ago. They were also among the most likely to think the US had lost out from free trade deals, that government benefits were too readily available, that social liberalism, globalisation, and immigration had been a force for ill, and that feminism had been a mixed blessing. Just under two thirds said capitalism had been a force for good, making them the most likely to do so, and they overwhelmingly believed the Supreme Court should base its decisions on the Constitution as it was originally written and that protecting the Second Amendment was more important than gun control. More than one third said talk radio was an important news source, making them among the most likely to say this.

Trump 95%, Biden 5%. 3% swing to Republican since 2016.

Fox News Militants

Predominantly white, Protestant, and male, these were the most likely to be retired and to own their own home. Two thirds identified as born-again Christians, and they strongly believed that religion was wrongly being driven out of American national life. Overwhelmingly identifying as conservative or very conservative, they were most likely to put up yard signs and to be pro-life, Originalist, support gun ownership rights, oppose same-sex marriage, favour smaller government, and think the US was the greatest country in the world. They overwhelmingly believed that people who work hard could be successful in America whatever their background. They were the most likely to think that life in America was worse overall than it was thirty years ago, and that multiculturalism, immigration, social liberalism, feminism, globalisation, and the green movement had been forces for ill. Two thirds said Fox News Channel was their most important news source.

Trump 99.5%, Biden 0.3%. 3% swing to Republican since 2016.

The Trump conundrum

DONALD TRUMP WAS THE first President to be defeated after his first term since George H. W. Bush in 1992, who was himself the first to suffer such a judgment since Jimmy Carter in 1980. But with a higher vote share and 11 million more votes than he received four years earlier, the 2020 election could hardly be described as a repudiation of the Trump presidency. He assembled the biggest ever voting coalition for a Republican nominee; indeed, the biggest of any presidential candidate in history, apart from Joe Biden. Clearly, there is a huge market for Trumpism. But what exactly is it? How far can it be separated from Donald Trump himself? And what do the answers tell us about the future of the Republican Party?

America the beautiful

We have seen in previous chapters some of the ways in which Trump and Biden voters differed from each other. While the pandemic was the most important issue facing the country for Biden voters, the economy and jobs were top of the agenda for Trump enthusiasts. While Biden enthusiasts prioritised race relations and the environment, Trumpers highlighted immigration and national security. Voters as a whole worried most about being able to pay for healthcare, crime, and losing jobs, but Trump voters were concerned about the possibility of America becoming a socialist country and the effects of immigration. While Biden enthusiasts saw Covid and climate change as the biggest threats to the US, Trump supporters cited excessive immigration and people with the wrong values and priorities having control of the government. When it came to issues of political principle, the question that most separated the two camps was over the Second Amendment: Biden enthusiasts agreed strongly that "it is more important to control gun ownership," and Trump enthusiasts agreed even more strongly that "it is more important to protect the right of Americans to own guns."

Further light is shed on these points when we look at how people see America in relation to other countries. More than three quarters of Trump enthusiasts said they believed the US was "the greatest country in the world." This compared to just under half of voters as a whole, and only one in three Biden enthusiasts, who were more likely to describe America as "one of the greatest countries in the world, along with some others." More than one in five Biden enthusiasts agreed that "there are other countries that are greater than the United States" – eleven times the proportion of Trump enthusiasts who said the same.

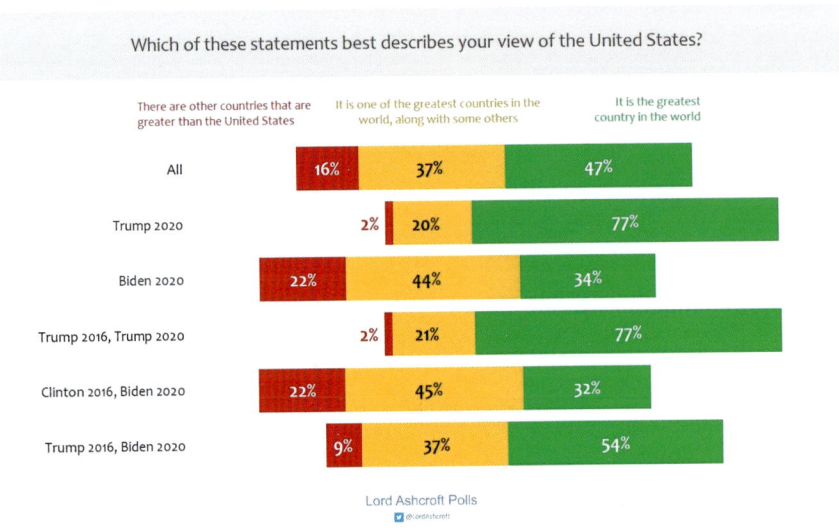

In our research as early as the 2016 campaign, potential Trump voters lamented an absence of American leadership in the world, and what they saw as its inevitable consequences. If the US doesn't lead, a Wisconsin voter told us, "nobody else who is palatable for Americans is going to do it… We're leaving the door open for other people to do it, and when we walk away, like Somalia, where did that get us? Pirates attacking our shipping containers as they're going across the ocean, and everybody's like, 'jeez, look at all these pirates'."

In 2017 a Trump voter in Texas summed up what he considered the sharply contrasting Trump approach to foreign policy: "Somebody has to be in charge, it has to be us, and that's what he's saying." Air strikes in Syria following the Assad regime's use of chemical weapons had been a case in point: "We had to get their attention. They'll think twice next time. I think he's showing them we're not going to put up with any crap."

Much about the divergent attitude to foreign affairs between Trump's supporters and opponents was revealed in my survey to mark the first anniversary of the 2016 election. Nine in ten Democrats thought Trump had a negative reputation around the world, and that this was bad for America. While half of Trump voters thought he actually had a positive reputation, a significant 36% thought he had a negative reputation but that this didn't matter. They welcomed his abrasive approach. "He's not a pushover," as one supporter put it in a focus group at the time. "He's proud of our country, he's not afraid to say it. Obama was apologising for our country."

This attitude in turn translated into a wariness of multilateralism and a suspicion that the US had been taken advantage of by international institutions. During the midterm election campaign, we found a majority of 2016 Trump voters saying they thought America had lost out from free trade, globalisation, immigration, NATO, and the United Nations, while a majority of Democrats thought the US had benefited from each one.

The Trump conundrum

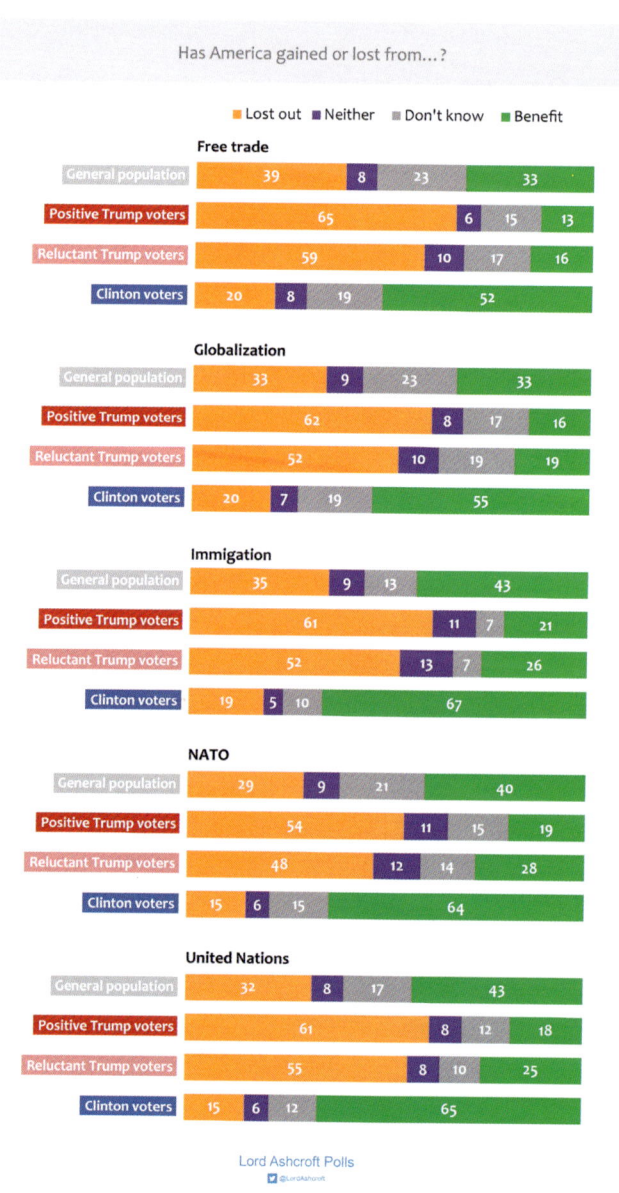

For Trump's opponents, his approach to diplomacy – which included sweeping threats, criticisms, and demands, often issued on Twitter or at press conferences – was among the worst aspects of his presidency. His own voters, however, were more likely to see his apparently erratic approach as being part of a considered and indeed effective strategy to prevent the US from being taken for granted. The achievement of a meeting with Kim Jong-Un and the subsequent release of American detainees from North Korea, the renegotiation of NAFTA, some success in persuading European allies to increase defence spending, and, later, the brokering of a peace deal between Israel and the UAE were regularly cited as evidence of his success on the international front.

This view of American greatness also applied in important ways to the domestic front. Asked how they felt about various propositions about the US, Trump enthusiasts divided in much the same way as other voters on whether life for today's children would be better or worse than it was for their parents, whether the changing economy brought more threats or opportunities, and whether life in America was better or worse today than it was thirty years ago.

One question stood out, however. While, by a small margin, most Biden enthusiasts felt that "in America today, people from some backgrounds will never have a real chance to be successful no matter how hard they work," the overwhelming majority of Trump enthusiasts chose the alternative: "If you work hard, it is possible to be very successful in America no matter what your background."

Trumpism delivered

In January 2017, Trump voters expected the incoming President to be more effective than his predecessors on practically all fronts, but especially on the economy. When I asked in a survey whether he would have more or less impact than most Presidents in a range of areas, "keeping jobs in the US rather than letting them go overseas," "the overall economic situation," and "creating new jobs" were three of the four objectives on which they were most optimistic; "preventing illegal immigration" was second on the list. They saw jobs and national security as the most important issues facing the country, and expected the country to be stronger, richer, and taken more seriously internationally four years later than it was then.

In focus groups in Macomb County, Michigan, which had backed Trump having voted twice for Obama, I found the new President's voters impressed with his early actions. especially the Executive Order restricting travel to the US from a number of largely Muslim countries. They were encouraged that Trump had already set about keeping his promises: "He said he was going to take control of the borders, and he's doing it," as one said.

Trump's flying start, as they saw it, only served to heighten expectations for what he would achieve in the following four years. Asked what they expected him to improve, one told us, "All of it. Taxes, education, economy… Nobody I know is happy with the way their life is right now. You're either paying too much for your medical, or you're paying too much in your income taxes – it needs to be fixed and he's going to do it. I got big hopes for that man."

A year after the election, I found 85% of Trump voters saying the President had made progress in delivering his agenda, though only a quarter thought there had been "a great deal of progress." Three quarters said they thought he had done at least as well as expected, including 28% who thought he had done even better. Only 12% of Trump voters who had expected him to do a good job said he had done worse than they had anticipated. In focus groups, his voters talked about economic growth and deregulation, and welcomed the decision to withdraw from the Paris climate agreement.

At the halfway point of President Trump's term, the country's two top priorities at the time of his inauguration – the economy and healthcare – ranked top and bottom respectively when I asked voters to rate his performance. Nine in ten 2016 Trump voters said they expected the economy to do well over the next year both for the country as a whole and for themselves and their families. In focus groups, they often spontaneously mentioned a thriving economy as being foremost among his achievements. This had also helped reassure some who had voted for Trump only reluctantly, if at all. "I thought he was a joke," a man in California told us. "But being a blue-collar worker, being a construction worker, for commercial drivers the work has tripled for me since he's been in office… Maybe Trump's immature and he's definitely not a politician; he's a businessman. Maybe that's what we needed."

66   The Trump conundrum

For Trump supporters, another issue – his appointments to the Supreme Court – earned him scores as high as those they gave him on the economy. This was especially true of those who had voted for him only reluctantly; as we found in 2016, his promise to appoint conservative judges and the fear of the court taking a liberal direction under Hillary Clinton had helped turn out Republicans who were otherwise uneasy about their nominee.

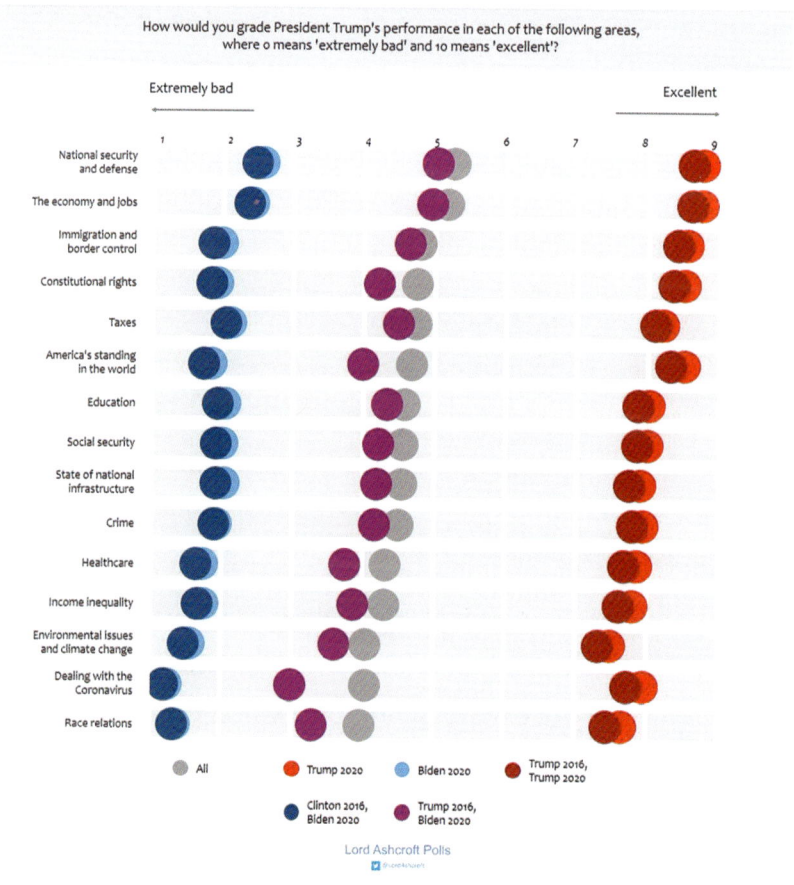

Throughout his term, President Trump's 2016 voters gave consistently high marks for his delivery of the policy agenda on which they had elected him. In our focus groups in October 2020, supporters spontaneously mentioned his record on the economy, deregulation, school choice, border control, tax, trade deals, foreign relations, bringing back jobs, the Supreme Court, criminal justice reform, law and order, standing up for America, and keeping his promises. In our survey during the campaign, I found nearly nine out of ten 2016 Trump voters saying they approved of the job he had done as President, including 61% saying they approved strongly. They gave their average likelihood of voting for him again at 88/100, with three quarters putting their chance of turning out for him again above 90%.

The man, the mission

Donald Trump's opponents believed his 2016 victory owed more to his personal appeal for certain kinds of voters than to any real matters of substance. But for his own backers the fact that he "understood that a large number of voters felt their genuine concerns and priorities were being ignored by the political establishment" was the more important explanation for his election.

As I observed from my research in 2016, this aspect of Trump's appeal had close parallels with the UK's Brexit referendum five months earlier. In both cases, many wanted a break from the political settlement in which their own views and concerns seemed to count for nothing. Many Leave voters in Britain, like many Trump-supporting Americans, thought life was getting worse for people like them, were unhappy with the level of immigration, and saw more threats than opportunities in the way society and the economy were changing. Remain voters in the UK were nearly twice as likely as Leave voters to say globalisation had been a force for good, and Democrats and Republicans split in the same way.

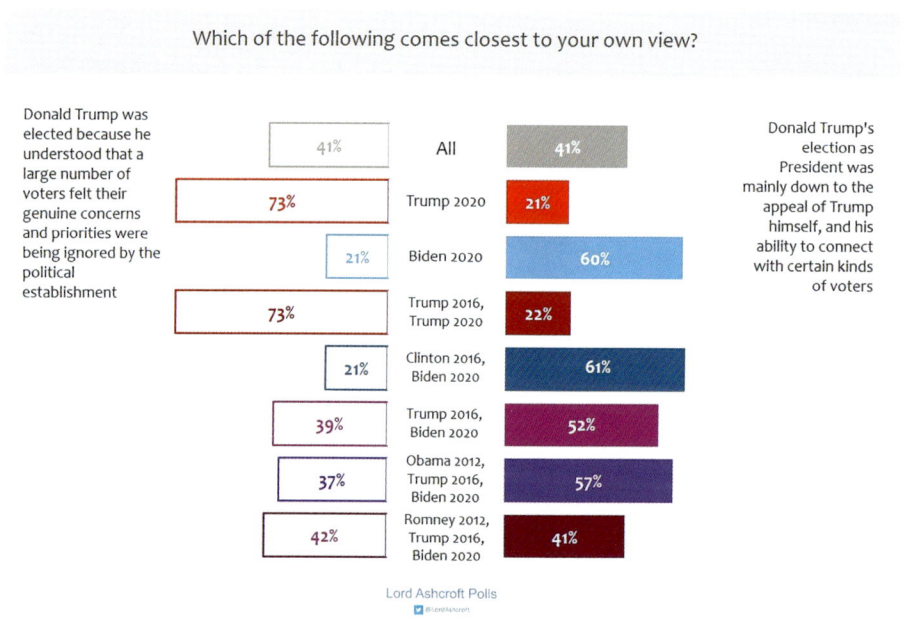

If the similarities in attitude were clear, so was the risk that both Trump and Brexit voters were willing to take to get the change they wanted to see. "We know we're not going to get any change with Hillary," as a man in Ohio told us the week before the election. "A lot of people feel like, let's roll the dice, and we're going to have to put up with a whole bunch of bad stuff, but maybe we'll get some things done with Trump."

Voters' willingness to distinguish between Trump's political aims and his personal conduct was a consistent theme throughout his presidency. Time and again during the 2016 campaign we heard people explain that they intended to vote for him despite what they regarded as his lamentable behaviour. "I wish he was a different man, but he's not," a voter in Pennsylvania told us. "But I don't want another career politician. I want change, and Trump is going to bring change." In our Macomb County groups, reflecting on the turbulent early weeks of the new administration and bizarre episodes such as Trump's claim that his inauguration crowd had been bigger than Obama's, his supporters told us they were braced for a bumpy ride. "I think because he's in office, that's what you're gonna get," one said. "Do I want that? No. Do I want the change? Yes."

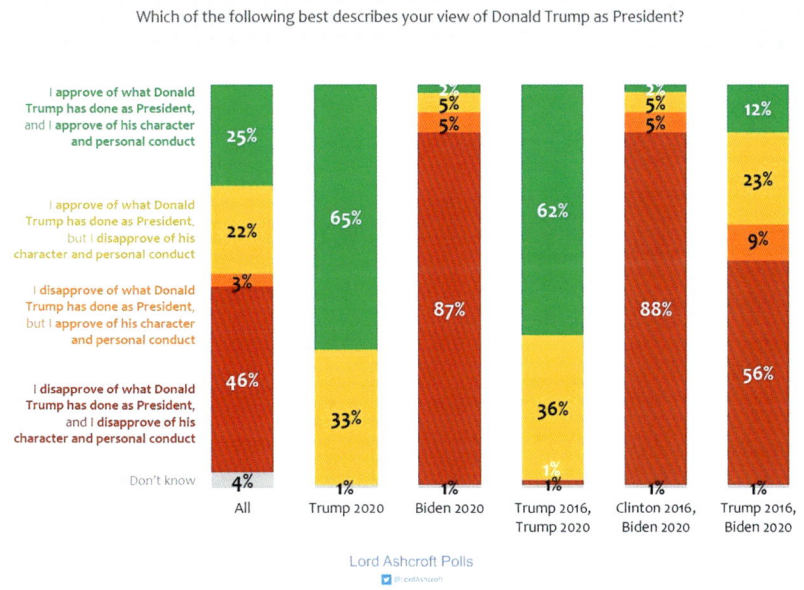

As time wore on, new revelations about Trump's conduct seemed to make no impact on his supporters. In early 2018, Stormy Daniels (an "adult actress," as some in our focus groups delicately described her) claimed she was paid $130,000 to keep quiet about an affair she had with Trump in 2006, but even the God-fearing voters of Tennessee and Mississippi were unbothered. "I want someone to work on our economy and protect our shores," said one. "I don't care about the rest of this stuff, because that's all between them and God. I'm not going to be that moral compass for him." After all, "we didn't elect him to be a saint, we elected him to be a leader."

During the 2020 campaign, one in three Trump enthusiasts told us they approved of what he had done as President but disapproved of his character and personal conduct. As we repeatedly heard in our focus groups, they regarded his antics as a price worth paying for the changes and policies they wanted. "Who says you have to like the President?" asked one who had turned out for Trump four years earlier and intended to do so again, despite having no admiration for him personally. "He's crass, he's rude, but he's standing his ground and he does believe in America." For another he was "like a great surgeon who is very arrogant and has a terrible bedside manner, but he's the one you want to do your surgery."

Even some of Trump's former voters disagreed with this assessment. Among those who switched from Trump in 2016 to Biden in 2020, more than half said they disapproved both of his actions as President and of his personal behaviour. But for nearly a quarter, the conduct alone had been enough: 23% of them said they approved of what he had done as President but not the way he had behaved while doing it.

Explaining their change of heart, such voters often told us in focus groups that they had expected him to tone things down once he was in office and had been dismayed that this had not been the case. "It's absolutely ridiculous. We knew we weren't getting a professional with him, but he's taken unprofessionalism to an entirely new level," said one. "I guess I expect the President to have some respect for the job," as another put it. "It's not good enough to be able to say, well, that's him." One remarked, "I grew up respecting people like Reagan, and my family listened when it was the debates or the state of the union or something the President said. Now it's like watching *The Jerry Springer Show*." The first televised debate of the 2020 campaign, in which Trump had been in particularly Trumpian form, had been a depressing experience for some of these voters. "I'm 51% for Trump but I pray Biden will show me something that will please make me change that," one woman told us afterwards. "I don't want a TV show running for another four years in my life, no sir."

Some who had switched to Trump having backed Obama in 2012 complained that his continued antics meant they had had the downside of his presidency but not the upside they were expecting. "We voted for change. We thought he was going to come in and buck the political system and not play this left versus right game that we're seeing now," said one. "I thought he would rise to the occasion," said another who had liked Trump's promised policy direction but not his character. "I thought he would elevate himself to the office and he actually wanted to do things for the people. Then it just seemed like a circus, and it's accelerating."

The Covid test

For many voters, President Trump's personal behaviour was tolerable so long as it was merely a sideshow. With the advent of the Covid pandemic, however, the interplay between personality and presidential action was brought into sharp focus.

Some people who had until then stuck with Trump despite their reservations told us they had been dismayed by his performances at the daily press conferences at the height of the crisis. "He's missing the compassion gene," one wavering voter told us in March. "He reads bullet points and then goes off on a tangent about how rich he is and how he doesn't need a pay check. It's not what we really want to hear right now." "It's almost painful to watch," another agreed. "I have to change the channel." Whoever was in charge would have struggled, but "he just comes across as too defiant to want to take advice from anybody, the medical profession. His ego just gets in the way the whole time." People were "looking for a consoler-in-chief, and that's just not his personality."

Many lamented what they saw as a lack of national leadership. "You don't know who's in charge, who is the adult in the room," as one put it. They felt the President had been wrong to downplay the seriousness of the situation rather than underlining its dangers, and his references to the "Chinese virus" were considered very unhelpful even by some who thought they contained an element of truth.

Some 2016 Trump voters who had already begun to have doubts said his handling of the pandemic had been the final straw. "The first three years, I could easily say the good outweighed the bad because the economy was getting better. It's the lack of response to the pandemic. It's him contracting the virus himself and still downplaying it," said one who now discounted voting for Trump again. "I found it very disappointing. I don't think it was a hoax, I don't think it's something you drink Clorox bleach for." Another added, "He dropped the ball bigtime, not only playing it down but making fun and making racial jokes about where it came from. It's not appropriate when you're the leader of the country."

They often felt that Trump's handling of the crisis had been emblematic of his presidency, or that his ego and behaviour had prevented progress or even cost lives. Typically, the President "thought he knew better than people who spent their entire lives studying this stuff. And he was wrong about that." He had wanted to appear "like he's bigger than the virus, he's going to beat it. And he's surrounded by yes-men. He's fine with a doctor standing next to him until they disagree one time, then all of a sudden they're gone." The President had "basically encouraged his followers to come out and be in close contact and not wear masks. He's helped kill a lot of people, I think."

His evident aversion to mask wearing and social distancing meant there was strikingly little sympathy for President Trump when he contracted the virus himself. "With him getting Covid and his blatant disrespect for wearing masks, it just seems like he could have avoided that and avoided other people getting it as well." Trump had had "a kind of karma experience. He said it was a hoax and now he's a super-spreader." His declarations that people should not be afraid of Covid also infuriated some otherwise potentially supportive voters. "I'm a mother of eight kids," said one. "I do have something to be afraid of. If I get sick, I can't care for my children, if my husband gets sick, he can't work. We can't afford these Molotov cocktails of medication that he got in hospital to make him feel better."

In our October poll, voters as a whole gave President Trump lower marks for his handling of the Covid pandemic than for any other aspect of his job. Trump–Biden switchers rated his management of the crisis even lower at 30/100 – which was itself more than double the score awarded by 2016 non-voters who planned to vote for Biden (13/100). Even 2020 Trump enthusiasts gave him slightly less stratospheric marks in this area than they did in most others.

However, it was striking in our research that the most critical were those who had already become disillusioned with the Trump presidency by the time the current crisis began to unfold. For them, his familiar flaws had simply become more grating while the change he promised had yet to materialise for them personally. His response to Covid-19 simply encapsulated why they were disappointed with him: while they hoped he would surround himself with experts having drained the swamp of Washington politics, he seemed to be ignoring or undermining the people whose advice ought to be holding sway.

74   The Trump conundrum

Voters sticking with Trump tended to say he was doing as well as any other leader could in the circumstances. In trying to play down the risks "he was trying to avoid panic." If the crisis had not shown him in his best light, this was because it had highlighted character traits that they had decided to discount as long ago as 2016. He might be self-indulgent and undiplomatic, they argued, but sooner or later the country was going to have to get back to business, and, for them, Donald Trump was the man to make that happen. "Who do you want there to rebuild the country?" as a man in Tampa put it. "To me, that's going to be his greatest opportunity to shine."

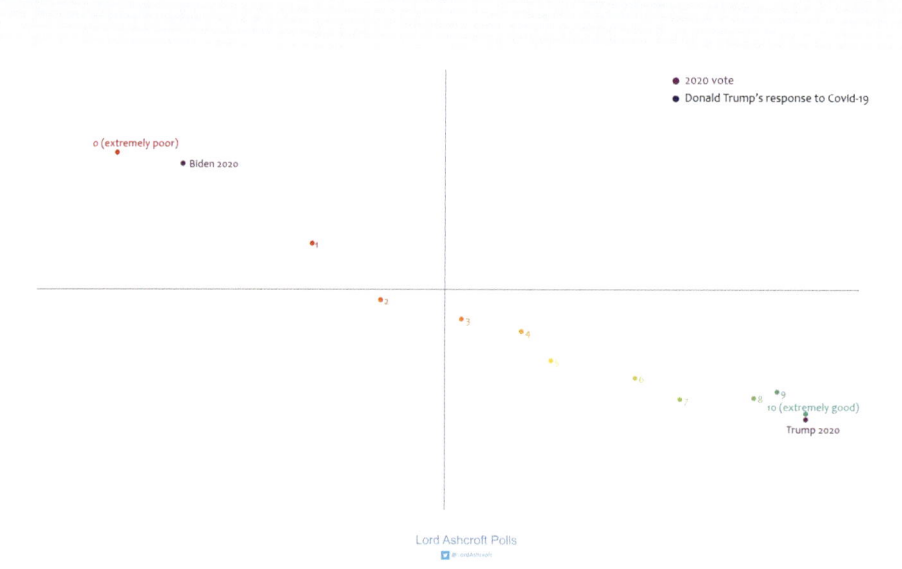

By the October campaign, the rating people gave Trump for his handling of the pandemic was closely related to their propensity to vote for him. As our map shows, the lower the mark they were prepared to give him, the closer they were to Biden-supporting territory, and vice versa. Judging by the response in our groups, however, people's assessment of Trump's Covid performance was more a function of their political affiliation than a driver of it.

A feature, not a bug

Donald Trump's abrasive personal style undoubtedly came with a political cost. Many otherwise supportive voters were worn down and exhausted by the rancorous tone and the perpetual tumult that seemed to characterise his tenure: we saw earlier how previous supporters switching to Biden said they wanted a President who would create a more civil political climate and build consensus, even if they did not agree with everything he did.

But that is not the whole story. In our earlier question examining the trade-off between Trump's character and the things he did as President, it would be easy to overlook the fact that two thirds of his supporters said they approved both of his actions *and* the way he conducted himself.

There were several elements to this. One was that even if he sometimes overstepped the mark, these voters loved having a President who said exactly what he thought and refused to conform to politically correct orthodoxies that they themselves disliked. Things had "got to where you couldn't say Merry Christmas in America," a woman in Texas told us at the 100-day mark in the Trump term, exaggerating to make a point. "He's crude and rude, almost, but he's right about everything." His evident disdain for the #MeToo movement and his criticism of NFL players taking a knee in support of Black Lives Matter, while inflammatory, were quietly cheered. If things like this were condemned by celebrities, so much the better. "I'm tired of hearing what Hollywood has to say and what we should be thinking," a man in Michigan told us soon after Trump's inauguration. "I look at them as the carnival folk. They have their sheltered little lives in Hollywood where they live in gated communities, they really don't live in the real world… And that's another reason I liked Trump – he just tore Hollywood a new one." Nor should left-wing protesters taking to the streets throw him off course. "They're going to stomp their feet no matter what he does," as one supporter put it. "He could hand them a thousand dollars and they'd still find something to bitch about."

Trump voters also appreciated his willingness to go into battle on behalf of their values, not least over his appointments to the Supreme Court. During the 2018 midterm campaign, several voters who might otherwise have sat out the Congressional election told us they were so furious at the idea of unproven accusations of historical sexual harassment derailing the nomination of Brett Kavanaugh that they were spurred into action. "In our country, whether Democrat or Republican, or whatever nationality or race you've come from, you're innocent until proven guilty," one indignant California voter told us. "Now there are Congressional members saying you have to prove your innocence. Are you kidding me?"

For these voters, Trump's undiplomatic personal style was also the hallmark of the political outsider, another trait that weighed heavily in his favour. The fact that he was a businessman with a different approach to solving problems was an important reason for their high hopes. At the outset of his term, an optimistic voter told us "he's going to figure out how to wheel and deal, he's going to get through the red tape, he's going to figure it out, and he's not going to be talking, he's going to be getting it done." This was a recurring motif: in our survey in January 2017, Trump voters told us that of the various aspects of his new job, their highest expectation was that he would "make things happen and get things done."

Some, however, were concerned that his approach to governing seemed far from businesslike. "I figured he would be a bit more organised, at the least," one Texas voter told us early in his term. "If there was going to be a positive it was going to be organisational skills, was my assumption, and it seems to be absolutely not the case." A prime example was the failed attempt to repeal and replace Obamacare: "Why was this piece of trash put forward to begin with?" demanded one exasperated supporter. For others, though, the culprit was not the President but Congress: "Trump's been there a hundred days; Congress has had eight years to come up with a better option." In fact, such failures served to reinforce the idea of an outsider up against an entrenched political establishment that encompassed both parties. "I feel that Mr. Trump really hasn't been given a chance to do his job," as one frustrated supporter in Nevada told us a year after the election. "If I was a hifalutin' Republican Congressperson or Senator, I wouldn't want to have to rebuild everything we all worked together to build behind the scenes because this guy wants to tear it all apart."

Qualities for the job

Differing views of the qualities needed in a President provide further evidence of voters' differing priorities. Offered a selection of potentially desirable characteristics, more than one third of Biden enthusiasts said being "honest and trustworthy" was the single most important quality, followed by "they care about people like me" and "they will bring about needed change."

Trump enthusiasts also picked "honest and trustworthy" as the attribute that mattered most, but only just. Close behind was "strong" – a feature that barely registered among Biden backers' top priorities. Being strong was also more important than average for Trump-leaning voters who stayed at home or backed Clinton in 2016.

The Trump conundrum

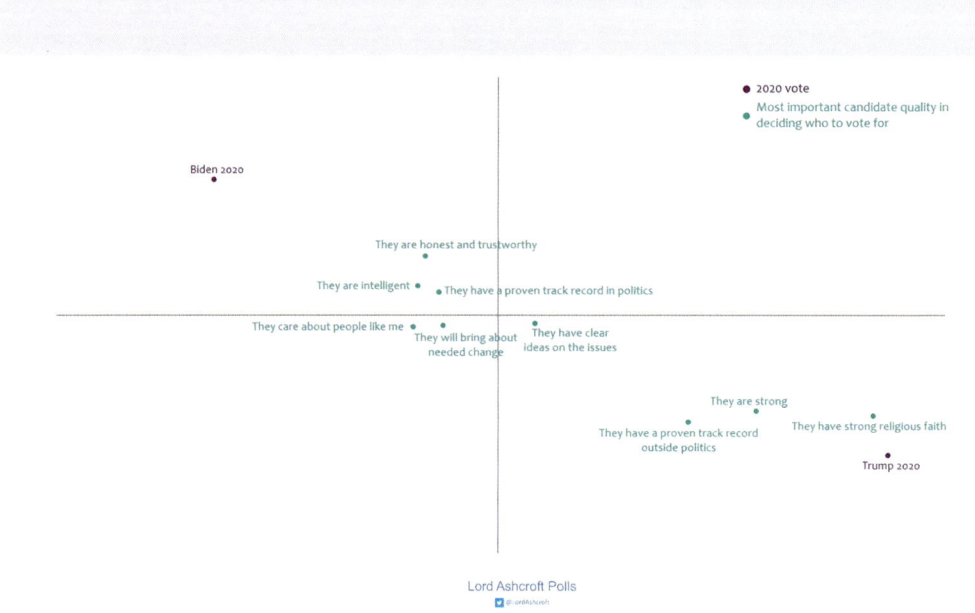

The map shows where people most likely to prioritise particular qualities are to be found in relation to the centre of gravity of Trump and Biden support. While honesty, intelligence, and a track record in politics were more likely to be prized in Biden territory, strength, a track record outside politics, and a religious faith were more likely to be valued by those closer to Trump (though few voters mentioned the latter two among their top priorities).

Incidentally, the idea of Donald Trump as honest or trustworthy would probably produce gasps of disbelief from his critics. But even if his statements sometimes fell foul of the fact-checkers, many voters saw him as honest in the more important sense that he spoke his mind and had set about doing what he promised – rare enough traits in an elected official.

Trump the Republican?

How strongly do you agree or disagree with each of the following statements?

Disagree ← → Agree

"Donald Trump is a typical Republican"

Disagree	Group	Agree
41%	All	51%
42%	Trump 2020	54%
44%	Biden 2020	50%
43%	Trump 2016, Trump 2020	54%
47%	Clinton 2016, Biden 2020	48%
45%	Trump 2016, Biden 2020	50%
37%	Obama 2012, Trump 2016, Biden 2020	58%
64%	Romney 2012, Trump 2016, Biden 2020	31%

"Joe Biden is a typical Democrat"

Disagree	Group	Agree
16%	All	75%
16%	Trump 2020	79%
17%	Biden 2020	78%
15%	Trump 2016, Trump 2020	81%
16%	Clinton 2016, Biden 2020	79%
17%	Trump 2016, Biden 2020	79%
16%	Obama 2012, Trump 2016, Biden 2020	81%
21%	Romney 2012, Trump 2016, Biden 2020	74%

Lord Ashcroft Polls

During the 2016 campaign, voters as a whole, and Republicans in particular, were much more likely to disagree than agree that "Donald Trump is typical of all Republican leaders." While this view was reinforced by some of his early battles with Congress, over time he has gone some way to remoulding the party in his own image – or at least, people are less likely to think of Trump and the Republican Party as two completely separate entities.

Even so, while most voters across the political spectrum see Joe Biden as a standard-issue Democrat, getting on for half of Trump enthusiasts still say that their man is not a typical Republican. The fact underlines that what attracted these voters to the 45th President was something other than the party label.

Evolution of a coalition

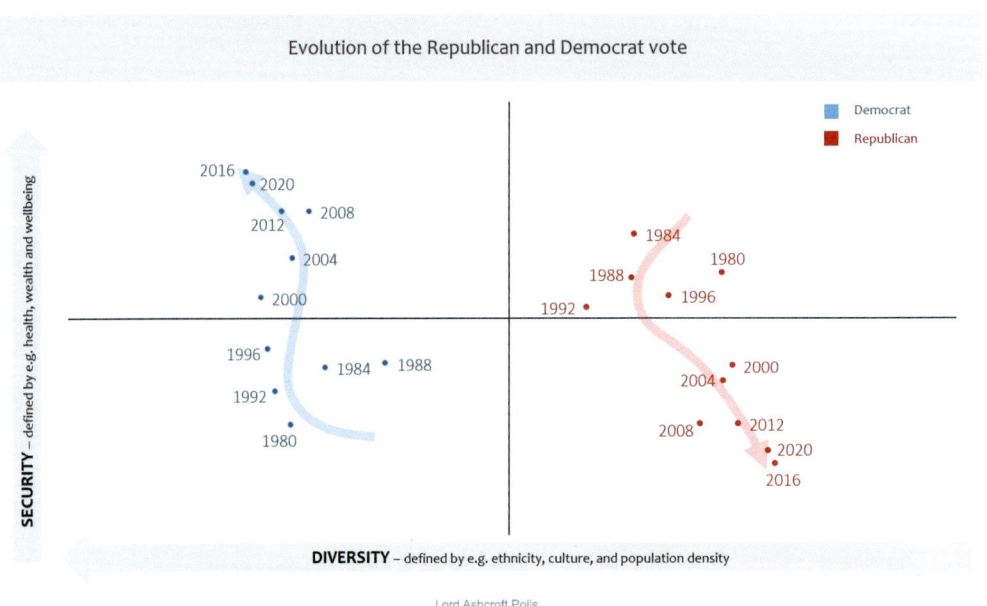

This makes it imperative for the Republican Party to recognise the new electoral coalition that Donald Trump built, and where it sits on the political map. The two parties in American politics have always drawn the base of their support from very different constituencies, but over the last forty years that fault-line has shifted completely. On this map, the vertical axis represents security, in terms of things like health, income and occupation – the higher up, the more secure. The horizontal axis represents diversity, which includes factors like ethnicity and population density – the further to the left, the more diverse. All these measures are derived from census data.

While always being rooted in more diverse populations, in economic terms the Democratic vote has grown steadily more upscale, to the point where its core is to be found in the high-security, high-diversity top left quadrant.

On the Republican side, the opposite has happened. When Ronald Reagan was first elected in 1980, Republican support was centred squarely in the top right quadrant of the map, among high-security, low-diversity voters. Over the ten presidential election cycles from 1980 to 2016, this drifted down to the bottom right as the GOP's centre of gravity has shifted to less prosperous rural and small-town America. The coalition that sent Trump to the White House is different from the one that elected George W. Bush, let alone his father. The dividing line in American politics – which ran from top left to bottom right and now runs from bottom left to top right – has rotated through 90 degrees in the space of two generations.

Trumpism without Trump?

From the analysis in this and preceding chapters we know a good deal about this new Republican coalition and what makes it distinct. This, together with further evidence, point to some lessons about the GOP's future.

82   The Trump conundrum

As before, our political map shows how different attributes and opinions interact with one another. The closer the plot points are to each other the more closely related they are. This one charts the results when we asked how positive or negative people felt towards various individuals and organisations, and how these relate to their political outlook and support for either candidate in the 2020 election.

Not surprisingly, we see peak support for politicians like AOC, Warren, Sanders, and Pelosi close to that for Black Lives Matter, the Democratic Party, environmentalism, and feminism. In the opposite corner we see a cluster of points representing peak favourability towards Mike Pence, Ted Cruz, the NRA, and conservatism, all very close to the centre of gravity of Trump enthusiasts.

Equally striking is that peak favourability towards President George W. Bush, 2012 presidential nominee Mitt Romney, and Rep. Liz Cheney, who has clashed with President Trump during his term and subsequently became the first member of the party's Congressional leadership to call on him to respect Biden's victory – let alone moderate 2016 primary candidate and former Ohio governor John Kasich – is some distance from the hub of the record-breaking new electoral coalition that turned out for Donald Trump in 2020. This is further evidence of how the centre of gravity in the Republican movement has shifted.

An anatomy of Trumpism

Having examined the views and attitudes of the Trump coalition, and where it sits on the political spectrum, how can we sum up what it is that brings them together? Is there a succinct definition of Trumpism? Looking back at what he did, and what his supporters told us about his appeal over four years of research, the list could be said to look something like this:

Trumpism…

American exceptionalism
Constitutional freedoms matter
Positive view of American life and opportunities
Reject political correctness and identity politics
Lower taxes, deregulation, belief in business
Assertive and independent foreign policy
Willingness to tolerate friction in politics

First and foremost, an unapologetic belief that the United States is the greatest country in the world, an understanding that the US is unique because of the freedoms enshrined in its Constitution, and a conviction that these freedoms are important and need defending. A positive and optimistic view of life in America and the opportunities it offers, including the belief that with hard work it is possible for anyone to be successful whatever their background. Consequently, a rejection of political correctness and identity politics or any suggestion that what people do or think should be determined by their race or other personal characteristics. Support for low taxes and belief in the power of business to bring about improvements in life, without unnecessary intrusion by government. Belief in an independent foreign policy, wariness of multilateralism, and readiness to be assertive with both allies and adversaries. And importantly, willingness to tolerate quite a high degree of friction in politics in the cause of defending and advancing each of these principles.

These elements were an important part of what motivated Donald Trump's voters in November 2020 to become part of the biggest Republican voting coalition in history. It remains to be seen how far new leaders will be prepared to adapt them in the cause of maintaining and expanding that coalition, or if they will be able to do so – how far it is possible to have Trumpism without Trump. Then again, as one admirer mused during the campaign, "The silver lining is that if he does lose this election, he can run again."

Methodological note

20,190 ADULTS WERE INTERVIEWED online between 14 and 29 October 2020. Results have been weighted to be representative of all adults in the United States. Full data tables can be found at LordAshcroftPolls.com.

Throughout the analysis, "Biden enthusiasts" and "Trump enthusiasts" are defined as people who rate their likelihood of voting for that candidate higher than any other candidate on a 100-point scale, and who also give that candidate a favourability rating of 75/100 or above.

The political "maps" used to illustrate various findings from the research are based on principal component analysis. Each map shows how different attributes and opinions interact with one another. The closer the plot points are to each other, the more closely related they are.

Sixteen online focus groups were held between 5 and 27 October 2020 with registered voters in Florida, Wisconsin, North Carolina, Michigan, Georgia, Ohio, Arizona and Pennsylvania.

The analysis also draws on previous quantitative and qualitative research conducted as part of the *Ashcroft in America* project. Full details of this research can be found at LordAshcroftPolls.com.

About Lord Ashcroft

LORD ASHCROFT KCMG PC is an international businessman, author, philanthropist and pollster. From 2005 to 2010 he was deputy chairman of the Conservative Party, having been its treasurer from 1998 to 2001. He began conducting political research in the run-up to the 2005 UK general election; the findings formed the basis of his book *Smell the Coffee: A Wake-Up Call for the Conservative Party*. In 2010 he founded Lord Ashcroft Polls, which has established a reputation for insightful non-partisan research on politics and public opinion in the UK, Europe and the United States, looking in detail at elections, referendums, political leadership, party brands and the motivations and priorities of voters.

As well as *Smell the Coffee*, his political works include: *Minority Verdict: The Conservative Party, The Voters and the 2010 Election*; *Well, You Did Ask: Why the UK Voted to Leave the EU*; *Call Me Dave: The Unauthorised Biography of David Cameron*; *Hopes and Fears: Trump, Clinton, the Voters and the Future*; *Jacob's Ladder: The Unauthorised Biography of Jacob Rees-Mogg*; and *Going for Broke: The Rise of Rishi Sunak*.

Lord Ashcroft is also honorary chairman and former treasurer of the International Democrat Union, founder and chairman of the board of the charity Crimestoppers, vice-patron of the Intelligence Corps Museum, a senior fellow of the International Strategic Studies Association, chairman of the trustees of Ashcroft Technology Academy and a former trustee of the Imperial War Museum. From 2012 to 2018 he served as the

Prime Minister's Special Representative on Veterans' Transition. He was Chancellor of Anglia Ruskin University in Essex from 2001 to 2020. His other books include: *Victoria Cross Heroes*; *Special Ops Heroes*; *Heroes of the Skies*; *George Cross Heroes*; *Special Forces Heroes*; *White Flag? An Examination of the UK's Defence Capability*; and *Unfair Game: An exposé of South Africa's captive-bred lion industry*.

Ashcroft in America

Lord Ashcroft's US research began in the autumn of 2016 with focus groups in seven swing states. The findings from these groups, together with analysis from a 30,000-sample poll, formed the basis of his book *Hopes and Fears: Trump, Clinton, the Voters and the Future*, which sought to explain how the country had arrived at its decision, as well as looking in detail at the US electorate and the prospects for the future of American politics. Since then, Lord Ashcroft has continued to conduct regular polls and focus groups which, together with his interviews with prominent figures on the American scene, form the basis of his occasional *Ashcroft in America* podcast, which is available on iTunes and other platforms. He also writes about his findings in the UK, US and international media. Lord Ashcroft's research and analysis is published at LordAshcroftPolls.com and his Facebook page, *Ashcroft in America*. You can also follow him on Twitter: @LordAshcroft